CORONA, QUEENS

PHOTOGRAPHS BY CARA GALOWITZ

DCV

Design: Cara Galowitz

Essay: Adam Harrison Levy

Copy Editing: Howard Gotfryd

Image Editing: Max-Color, Berlin

Production Management: DCV

Printing and Binding:
Optimal Media GmbH

All photographs in this publication (including front and back cover) were taken in Corona, Queens, from 2013 – 2020.

Distribution and marketing:
DCV sales@dcv-books.com

ISBN: 978-3-96912-083-5
Printed in Germany

Published by

DCV

www.dcv-books.com

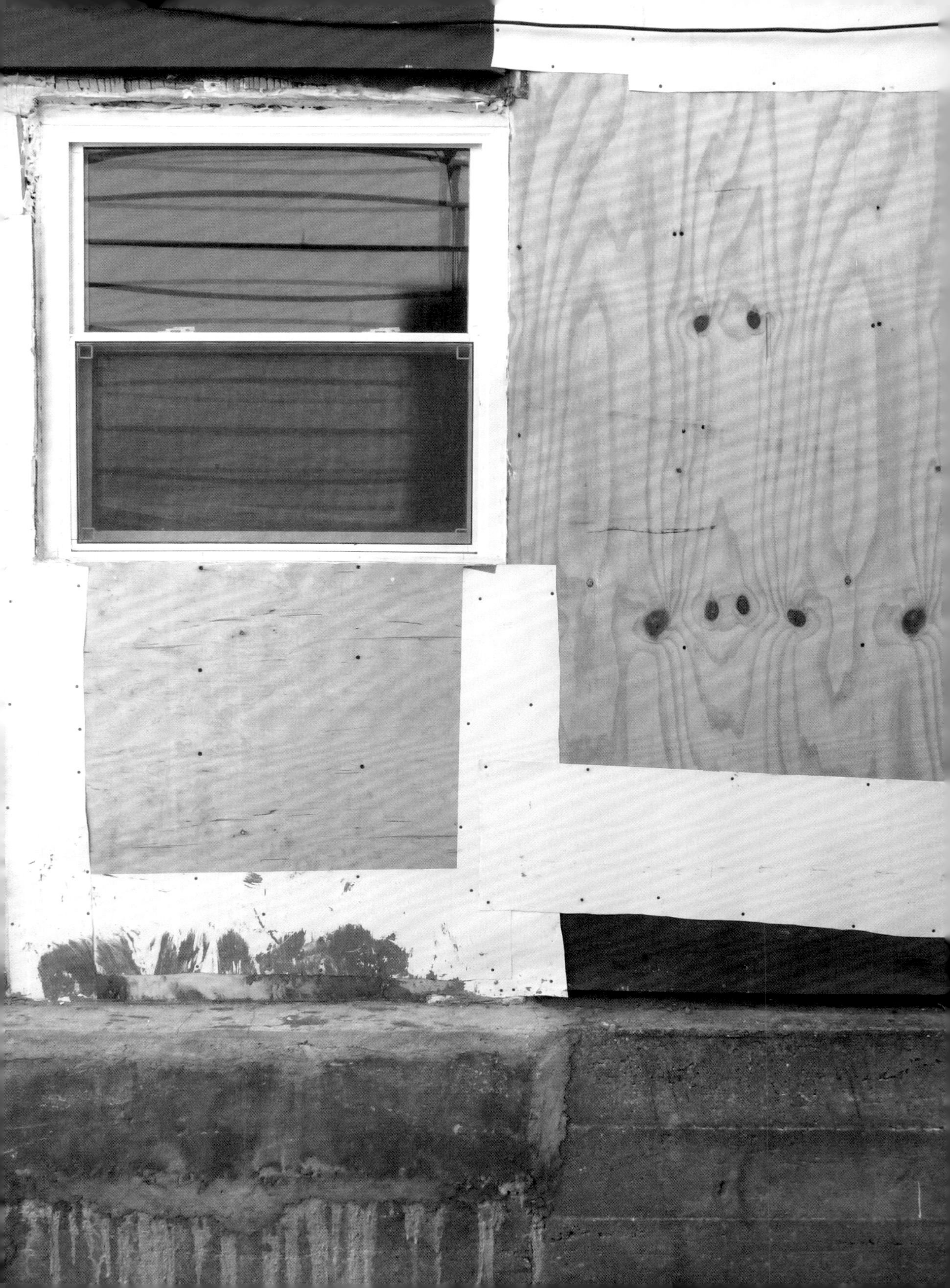

AN EXERCISE IN SEEING ADAM HARRISON LEVY

The spray-painted bride holds the hands of her corrugated groom. An array of sherbet-colored curtains shade the sun. A plastic swan nestles in vines. These are just some of the vivid images from Corona, Queens, that Cara Galowitz has seen, framed, and brought to our eyes.

For seven years, from 2013 – 2020, during her lunch hour, Cara walked the approximately four-mile radius of Corona, encompassing areas east from the New York Hall of Science, in Flushing Meadows Park, where she worked as a graphic designer, west to Junction Boulevard, north to Northern Boulevard, and south to the Long Island Expressway. She did this every day, except when it rained. This book is a selection of photographs from those walks. They are, she says, "an exercise in seeing."

Corona is a neighborhood that is layered with history, a patchwork of ethnicities. The newer arrivals are primarily Guatemalans, Ecuadorians, and Columbians who live among the previous wave of immigrants, including Mexicans, Asians, and Dominicans, who themselves moved into a neighborhood that had been primarily African-American, Irish, and Italian. Like the walls she photographs, with their layers of concrete, glass, and wood, this is a physical place that has been made in a continual process of improvisation and adaptation.

On a crisp day in February, Cara and I walk up Junction Boulevard. The sidewalk is lined with tables piled high with baseball hats, plastic key rings, and multi colored cell phone cases. The smoky smell of charred wood floats from a cart selling choclo blanco y mayonesa — roasted white corn with mayonnaise. Cara is dressed unobtrusively in a blue duffle coat and black Dr. Martens shoes. A digital camera hangs around her neck. She moves attentively, like a doe crossing an open field.

We turn east on 37th Avenue and enter a pocket of calm. We pass a red brick house, its yard piled with furniture — a chest of drawers, a broken bookcase. Has someone just moved out? Cara points to a cluster of mops piled haphazardly by a fence, their muddy strands tangled like hair. She laughs, enjoying the casual irony of this surreal image. "A lot of this speaks to my sensibility," she says, lifting her camera and taking a shot. She enjoys the visual humor of the street.

There is an underlying theme that inspired these walks, and which compelled her to document this changing urban landscape. When she was twelve, in the mid-1970s, she spent one and a half years in the Philippines and was struck by how people had to adapt to a Western-style modernity, how the old values and ways of living had to adjust to the new. She recalls seeing a small hut standing alone in a vast sugar cane field, with an air conditioner sticking out of its side.

Her work in Corona is the reverse, but with the same underlying impulse. Here, she is fascinated by how New York's harsh contemporary reality, in the form of our city landscape, is layered and transformed by immigrant cultures. She is attuned to the struggle of the people of Corona, their need, often in the face of poverty, to make things a bit more beautiful: a string of lights, a tree trunk painted emerald green, or a well-placed Madonna to watch over things.

In lesser hands these contrasts would be banal. But through off-center composition, astute framing, and an impeccable eye for color, she defamiliarizes the known. Her training as a graphic designer is clear: the inclusion of a dark shadow that curtains a brick wall and balances a larger block of stuccoed white gives one image a painterly abstraction.

Along with the whimsy and the beauty there is also darkness. Through the slats of a hoarding, intended to block the view into a courtyard, we see the "FU" letters of a macabre game of Hangman. This looks like a prison yard, a reminder of the dangers many of Corona's newer immigrants have fled.

Most of the people in these photographs are glimpsed through doors, gates, or glass. Some have their backs turned to us, others are looking away. Even those looking straight at us seem wary. These are sensitive portraits, respectful of their subject's space. It's the physical surfaces of Corona — the walls, car doors, and fences — that often carry the intimacy of character. The indented, cracked, and worn surfaces are like the wrinkles and lines of a face: evidence of time's tough progress. Cara brings the inanimate alive.

We end our walk near where we began, under the girders of the number 7 subway line. A man is passing out a local newspaper. He nervously slips a mask on and off his face. It's not possible to spend time in Corona and not be aware of the devastation that the Corona virus wreaked on the neighborhood. It's an unfortunate connection — the virus wasn't named for this place but it unleashed its vengeance early here, a contagion that spread through the crowded apartments and dense streets with deadly velocity.

Cara stopped taking her walks on March 11, 2020, ironically just a few days before New York went into lockdown — her exploration of Corona ended when the Corona virus arrived. One photograph eerily prophesies this devastating future: a handwritten "died" scrawled in red next to a mailbox out of which sticks a medical bill. The anguish of this image is counterbalanced by a photograph a few pages away: a soft spray of white roses, defocused behind a window, luminous in the shadows. It's a consoling image, a glimpse into a private world just on the other side of the glass, easily missed. This is what the best of these photographs do: they capture the overlooked beauty of things.

Adam Harrison Levy is a writer and documentary filmmaker. He has written catalog essays for The International Center of Photography's *Hiroshima: Ground Zero, 1945*, Pace Gallery's *Robert Whitman*, and the Deichtorhallen's *Saul Leiter*. His documentary films have appeared on the BBC, as have his interviews with a wide range of writers and artists. He currently teaches at the School of Visual Arts, in New York.

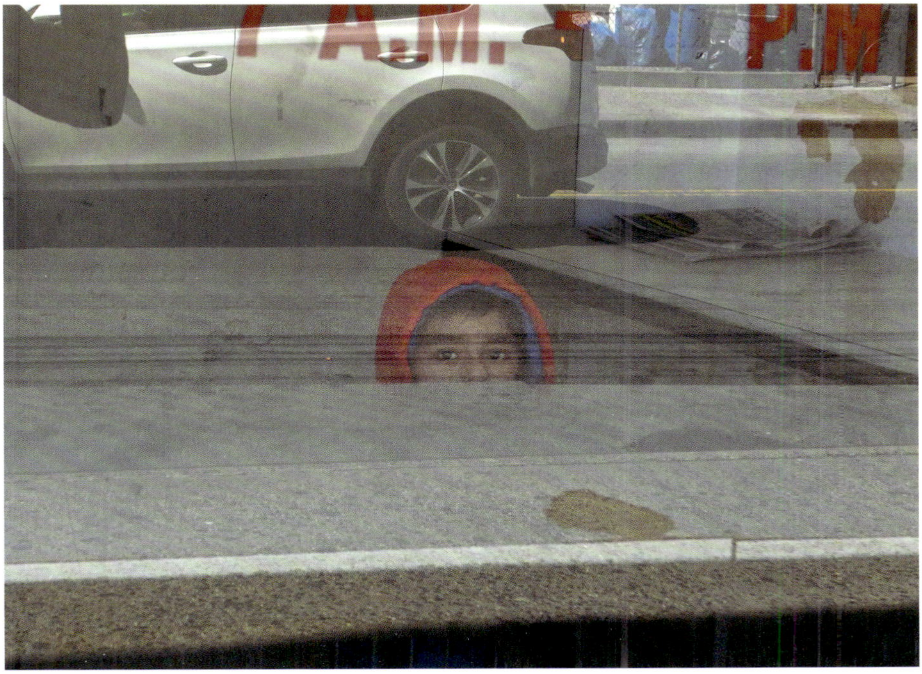
A.M.
P.M

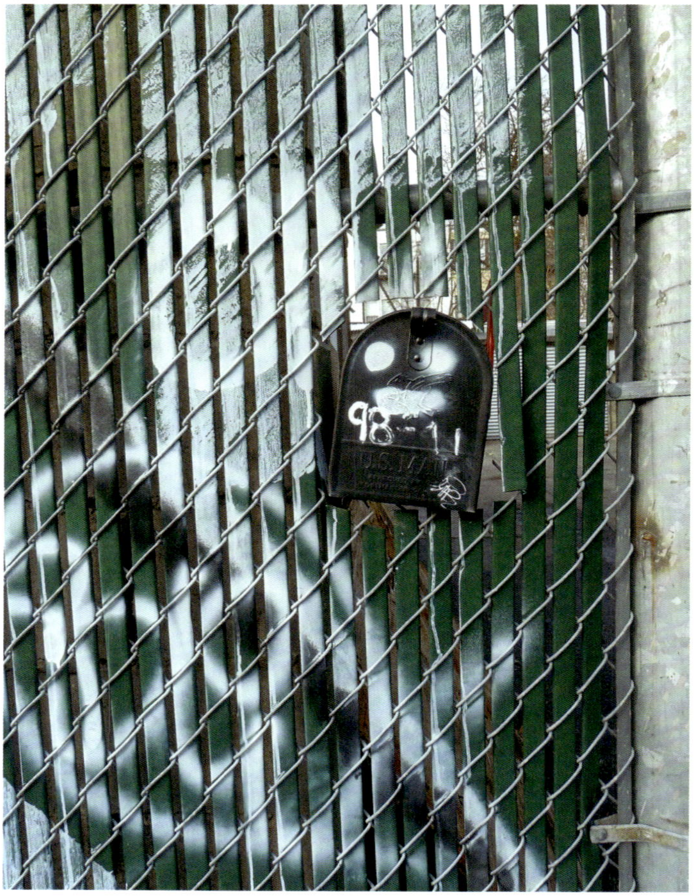
98-11
U.S. MAIL

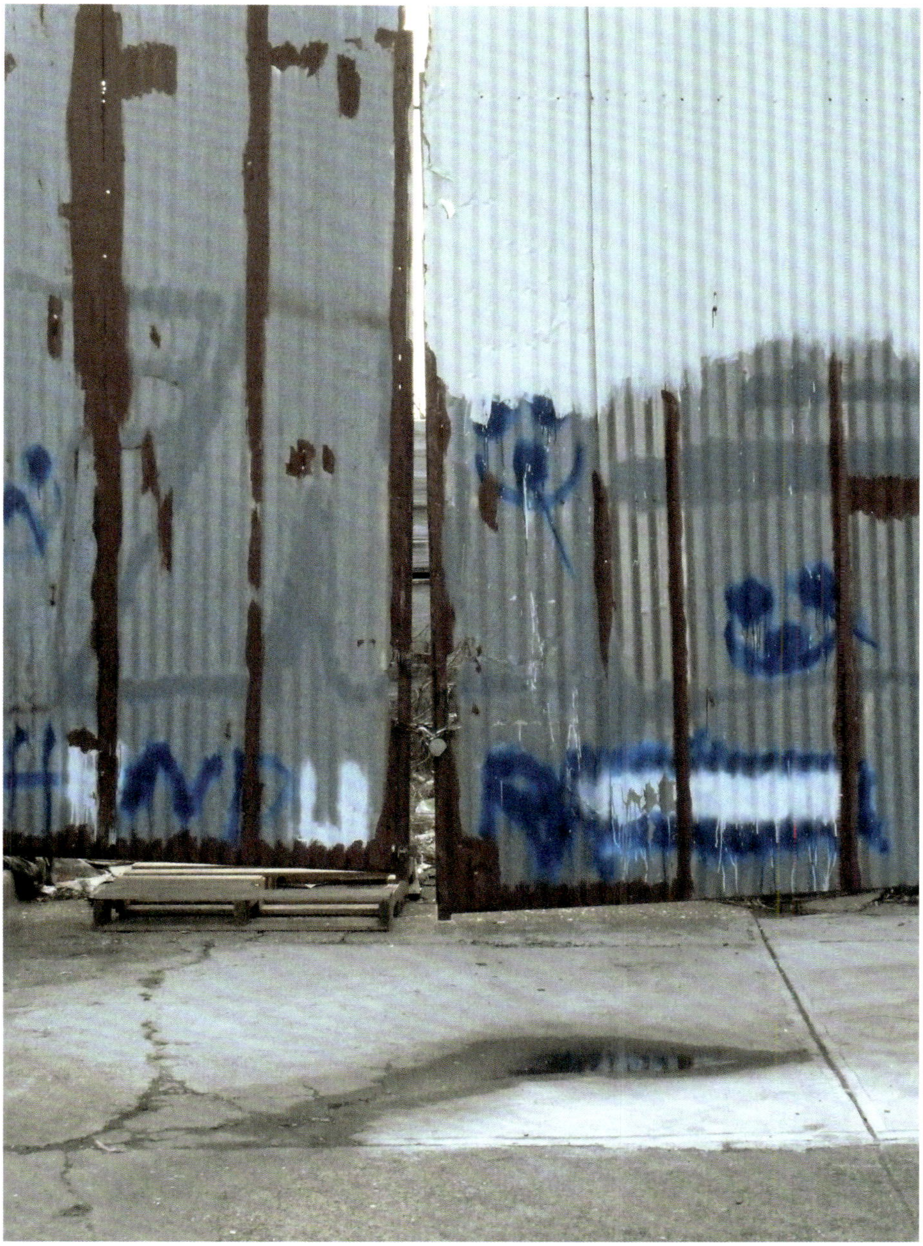

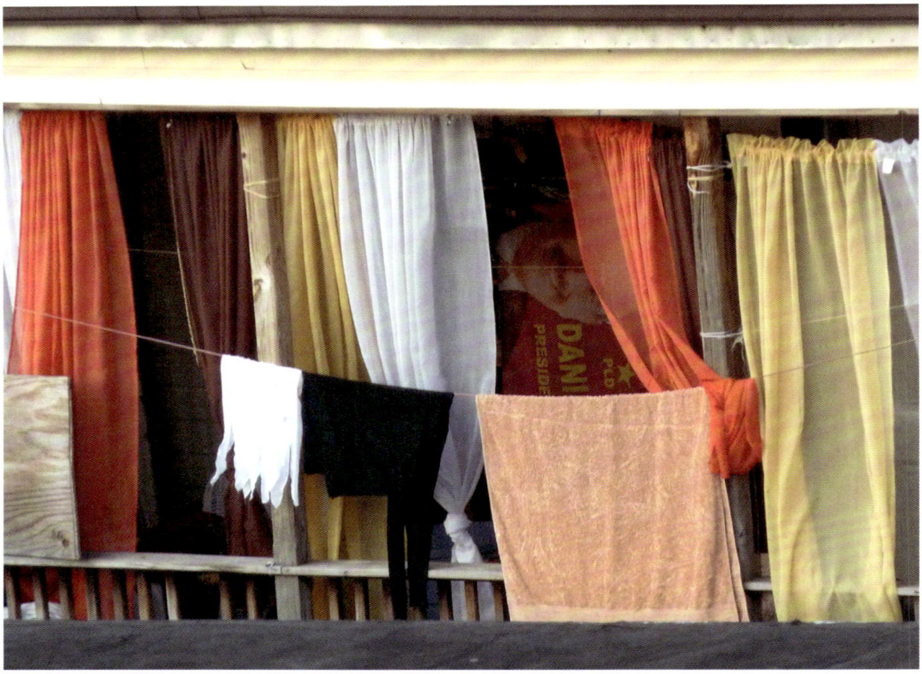
PLD
DANI
PRESIDE

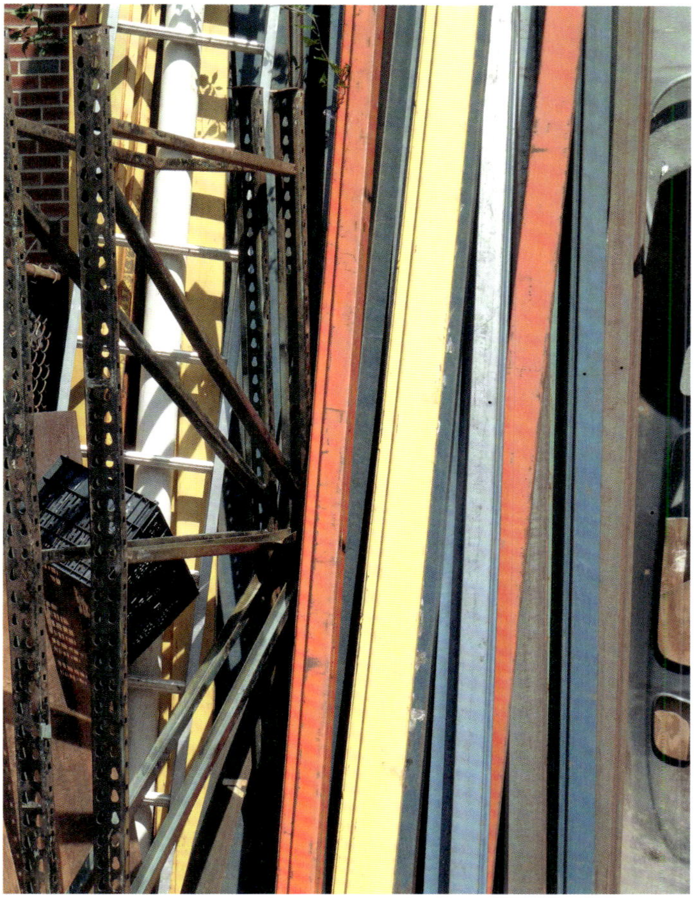

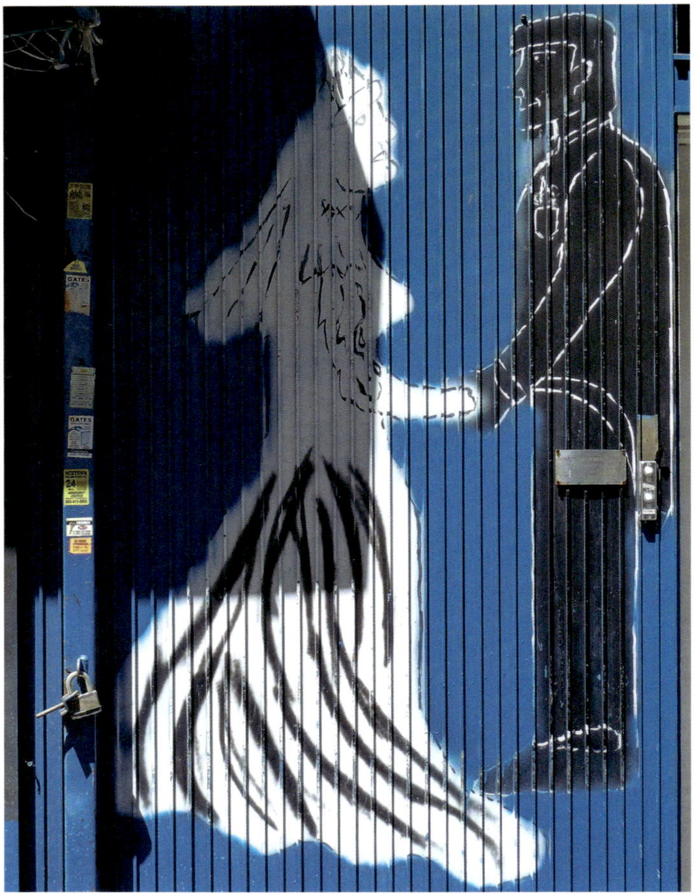

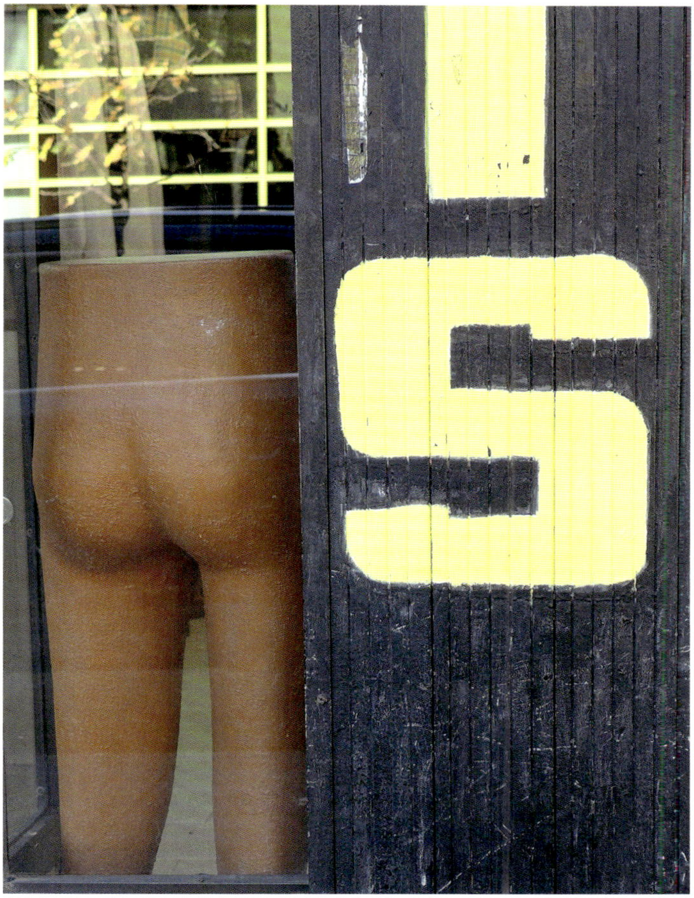
S

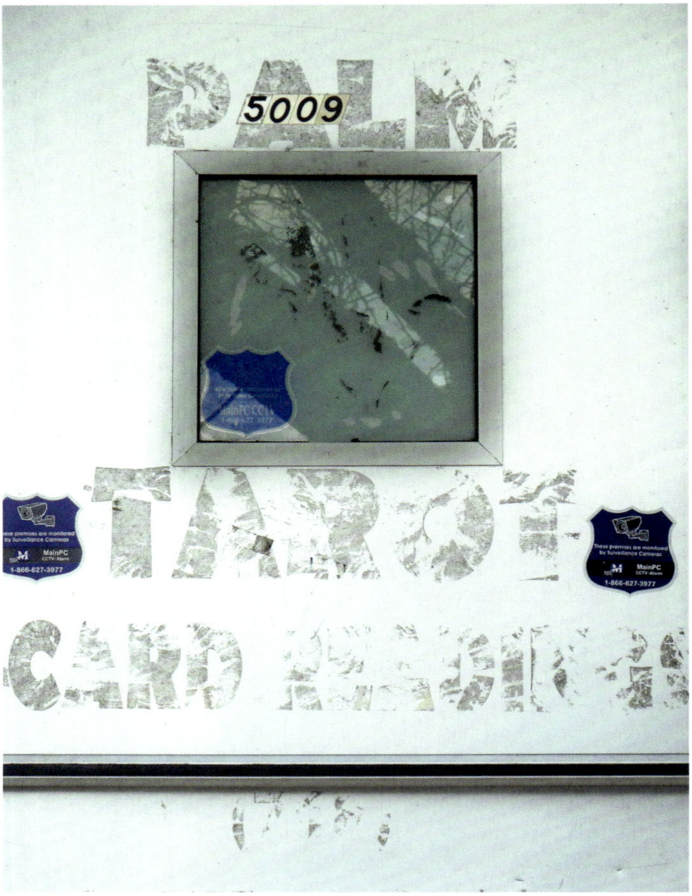
PALM
5009
TAROT
CARD
These premises are monitored by Surveillance Cameras
MainPC
CCTV-Alarm
1-866-627-3977

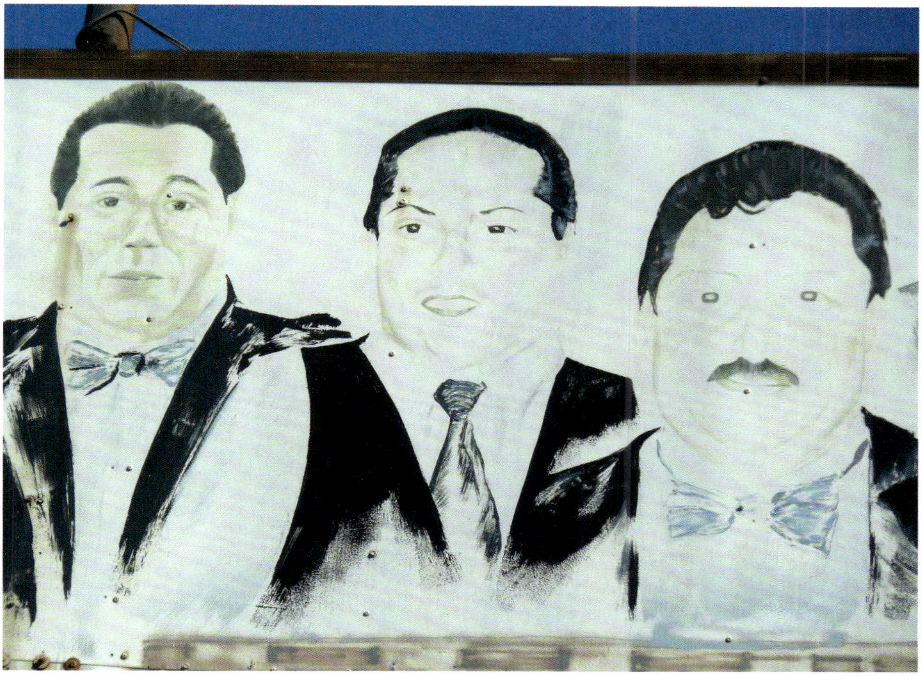

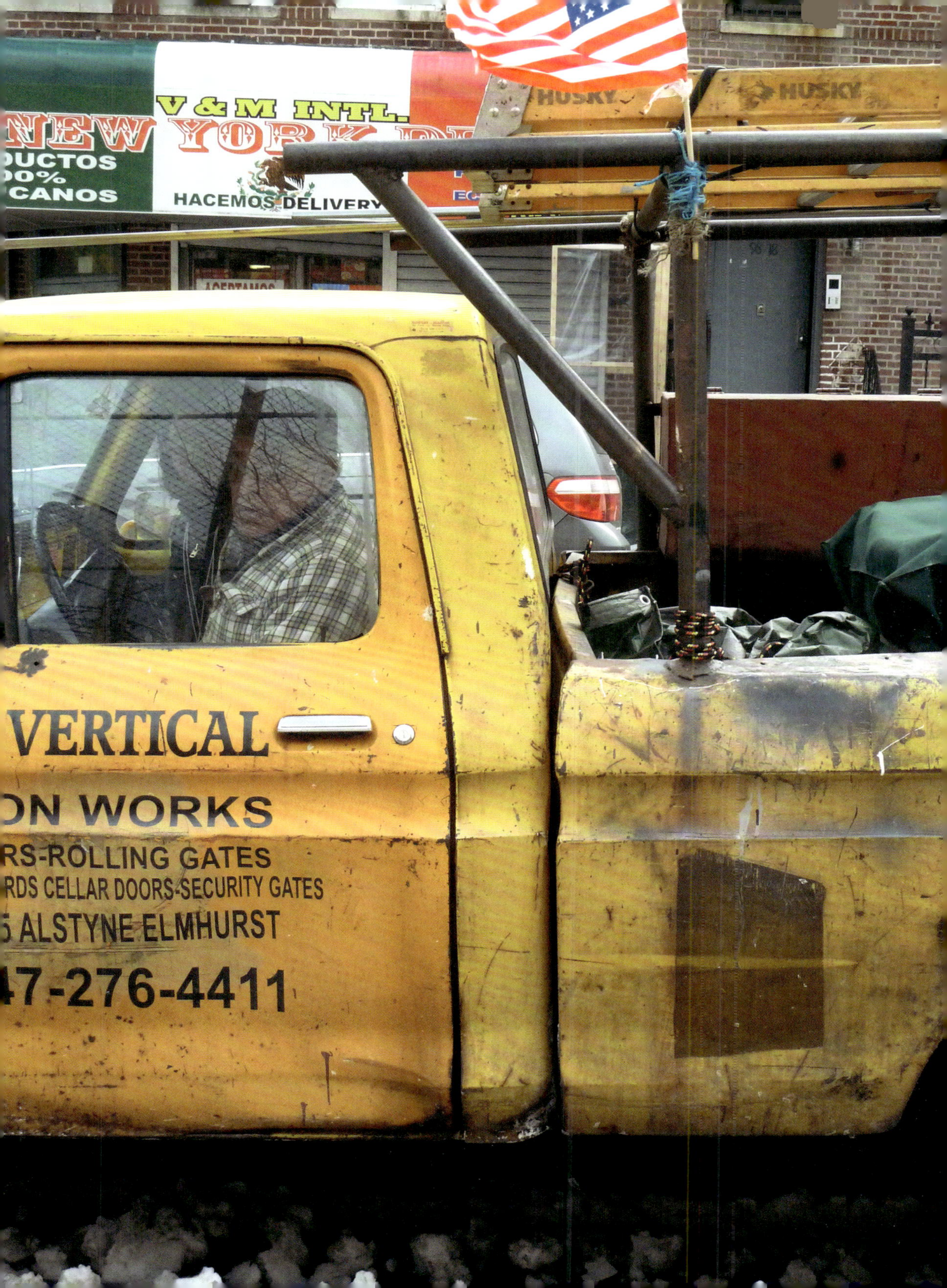

V & M INTL.
NEW
HACEMOS DELIVERY
HUSKY
HUSKY
VERTICAL
ON WORKS
RS-ROLLING GATES
RDS CELLAR DOORS-SECURITY GATES
5 ALSTYNE ELMHURST
47-276-4411

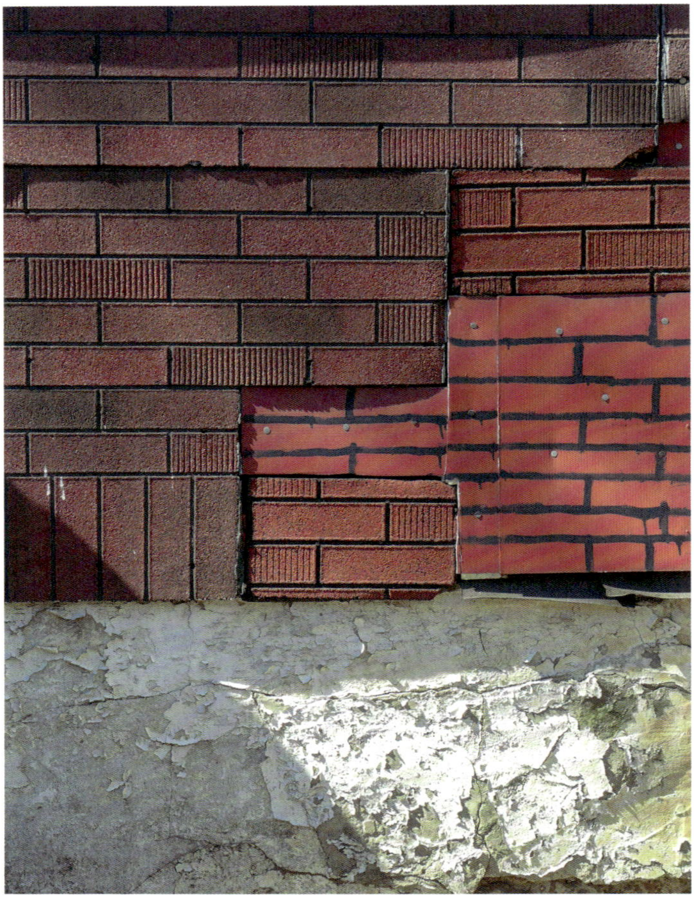

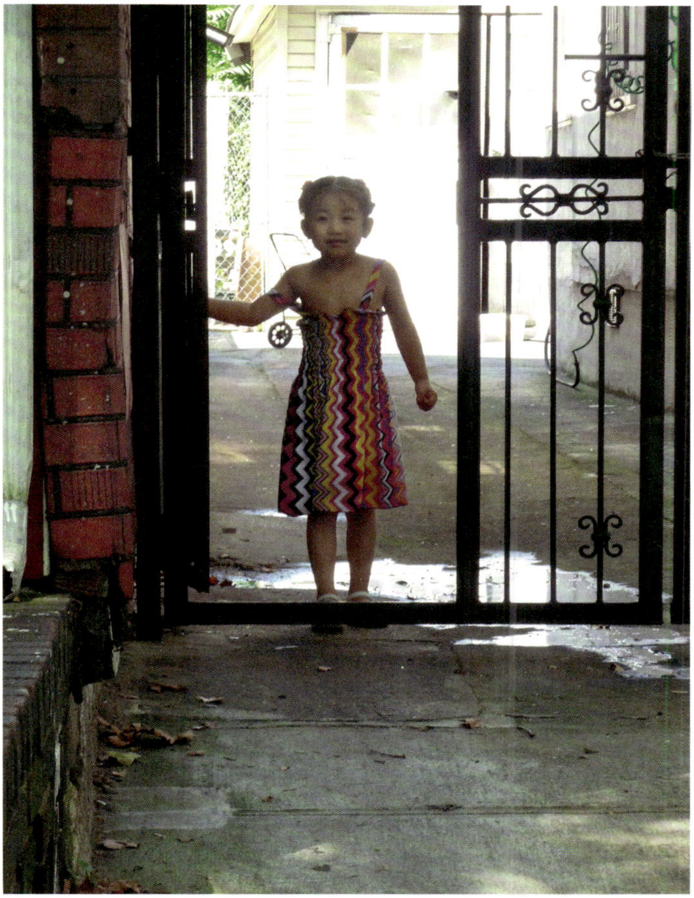

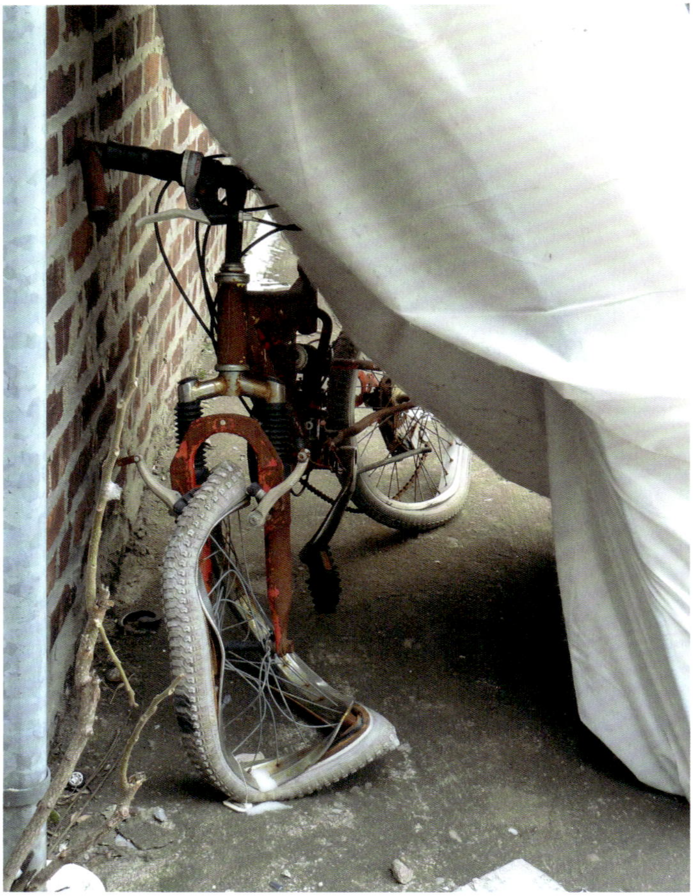

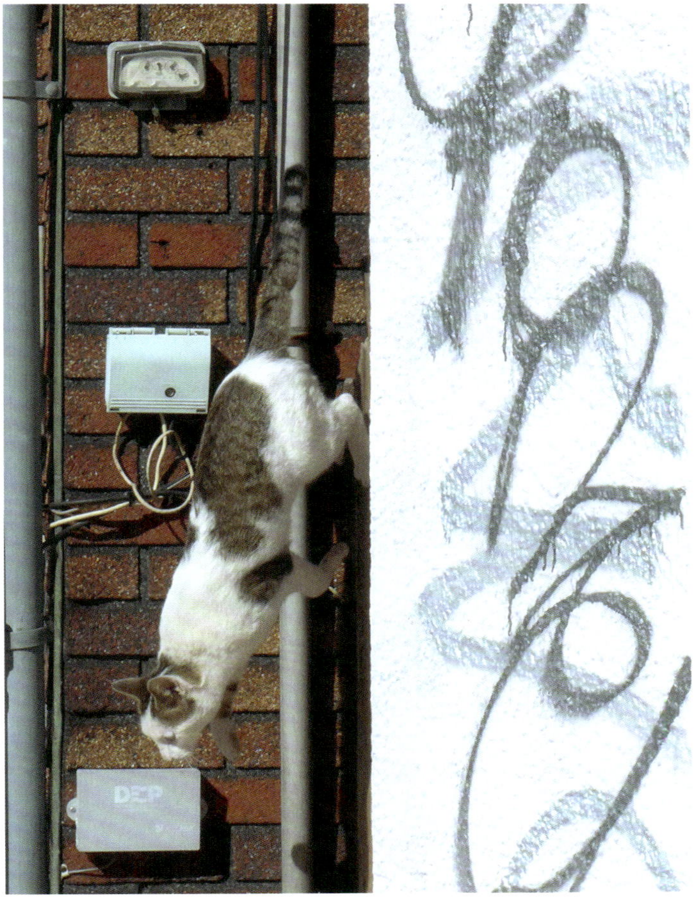
DEP

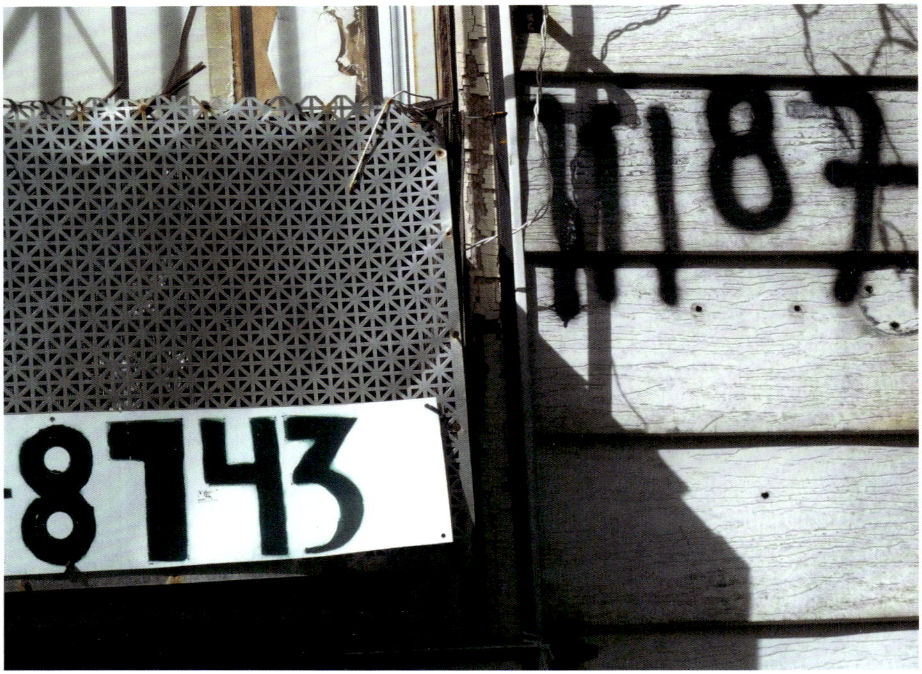
8143

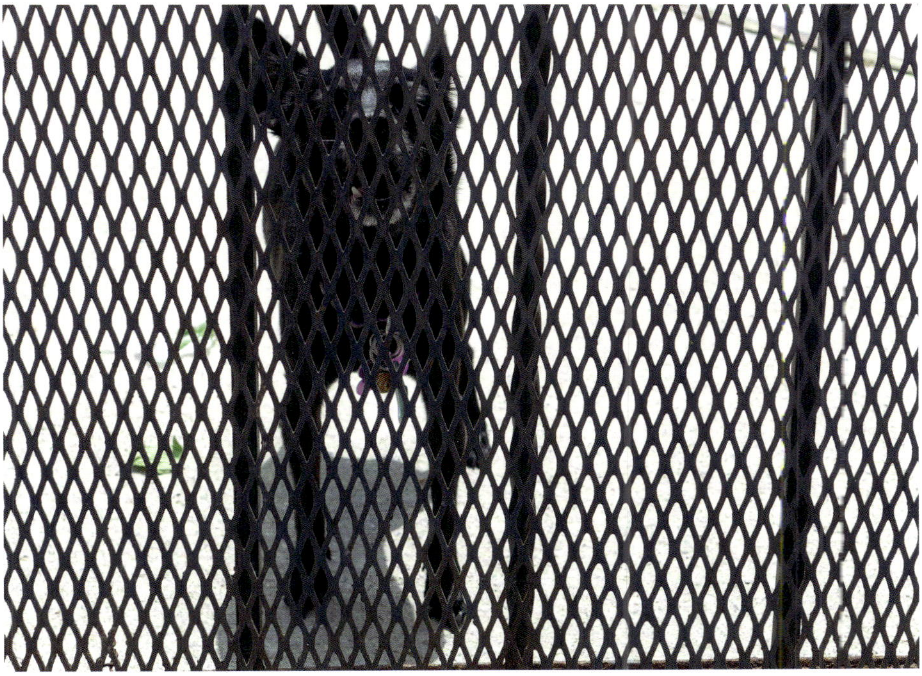

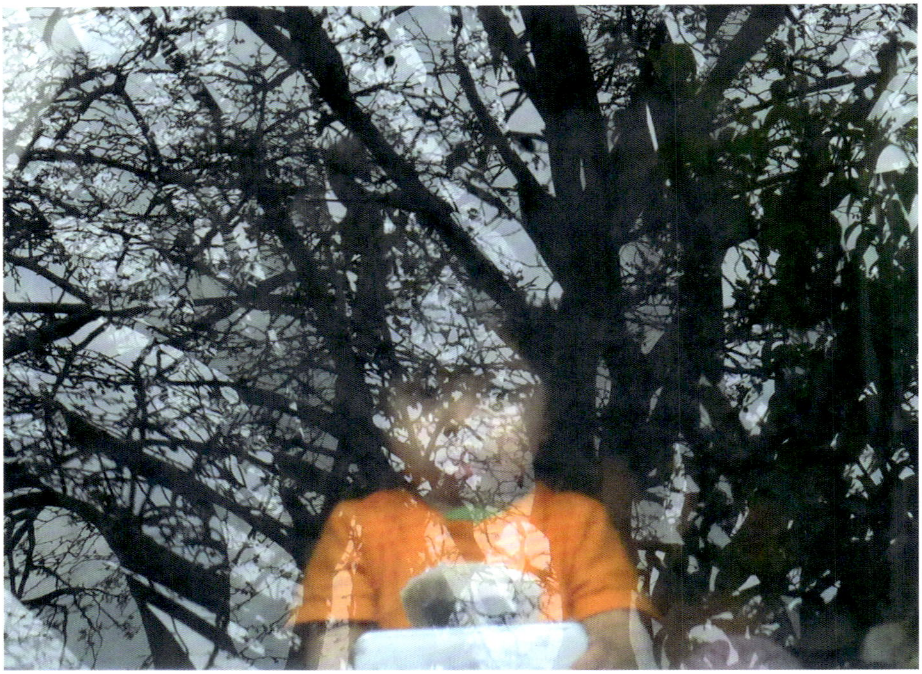

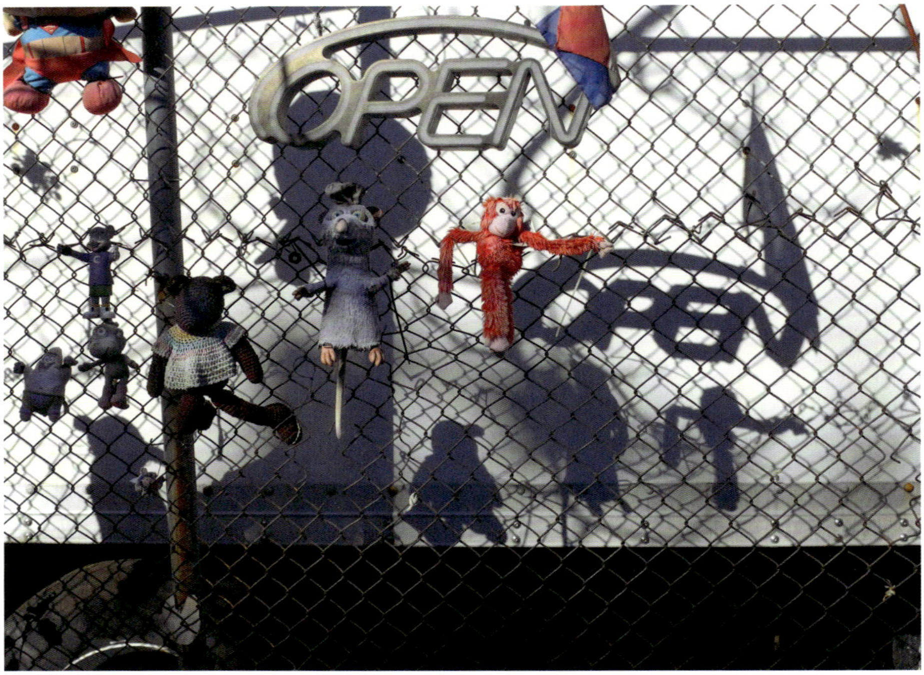
OPEN

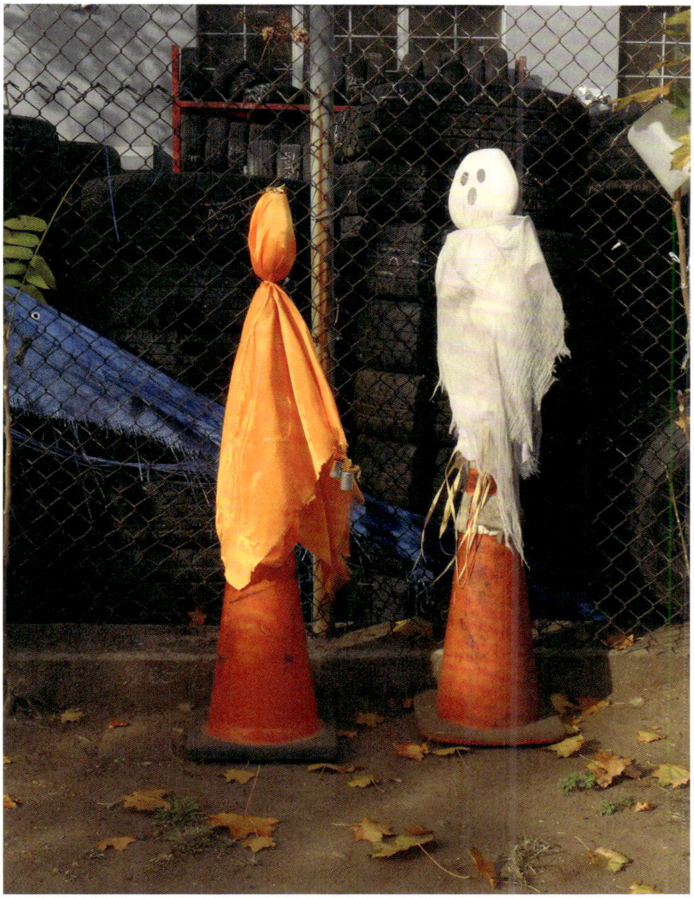

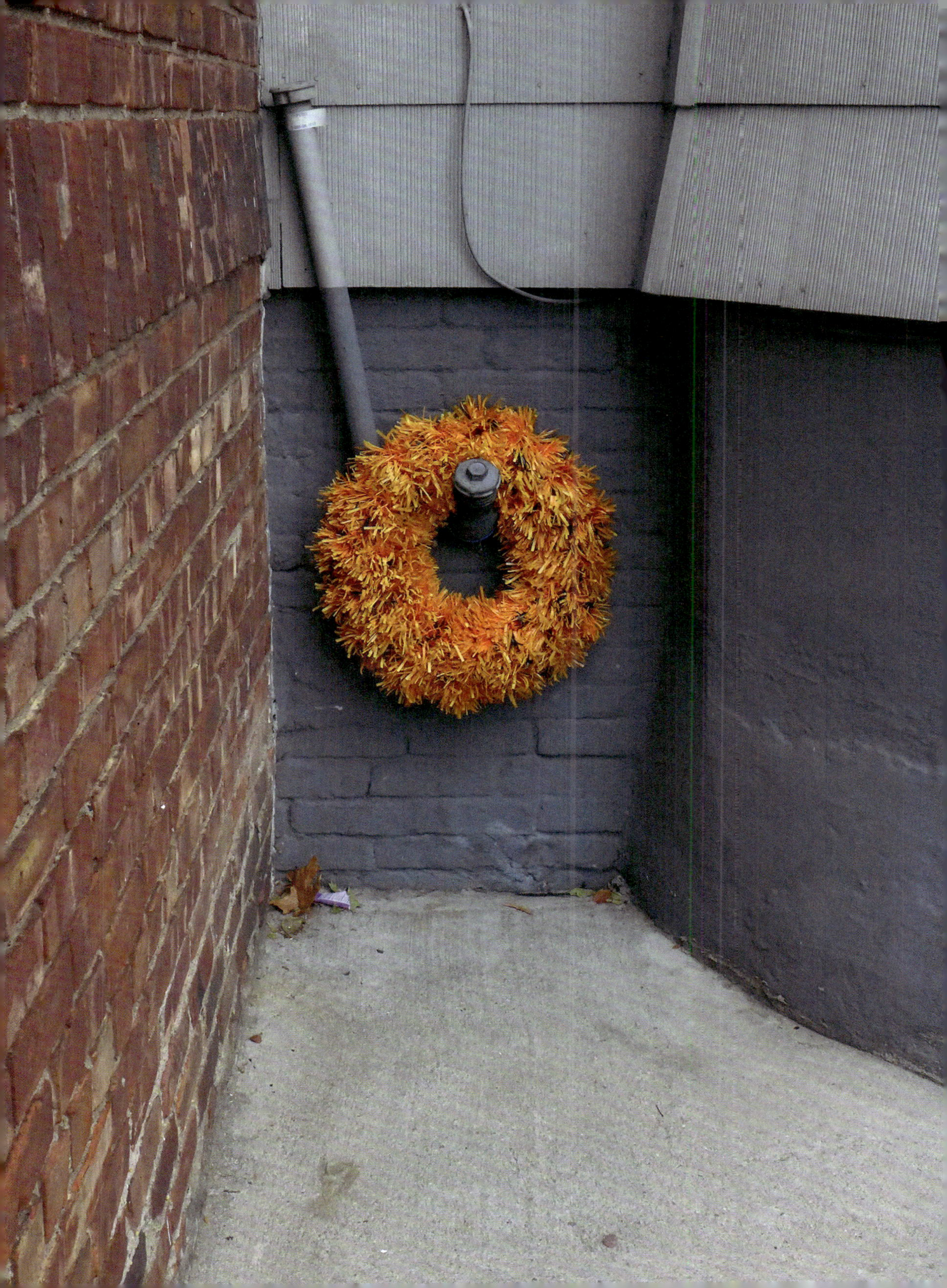

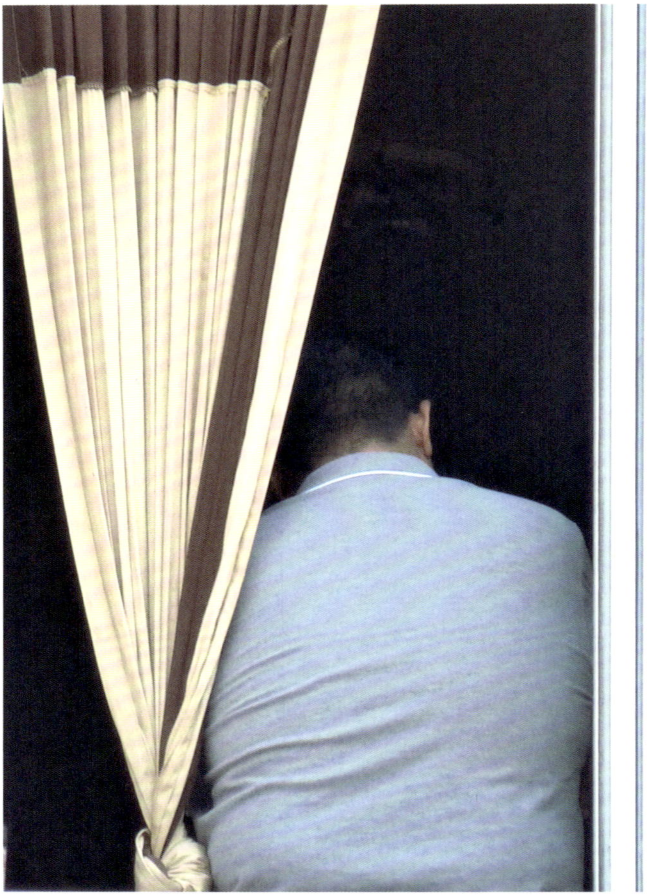

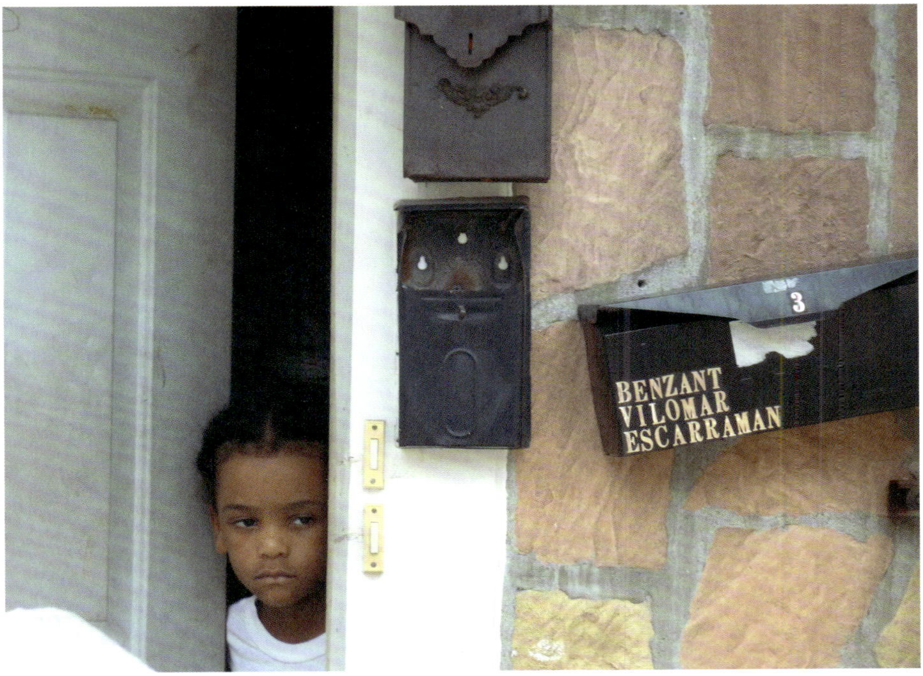
3
BENZANT
VILOMAR
ESCARRAMAN

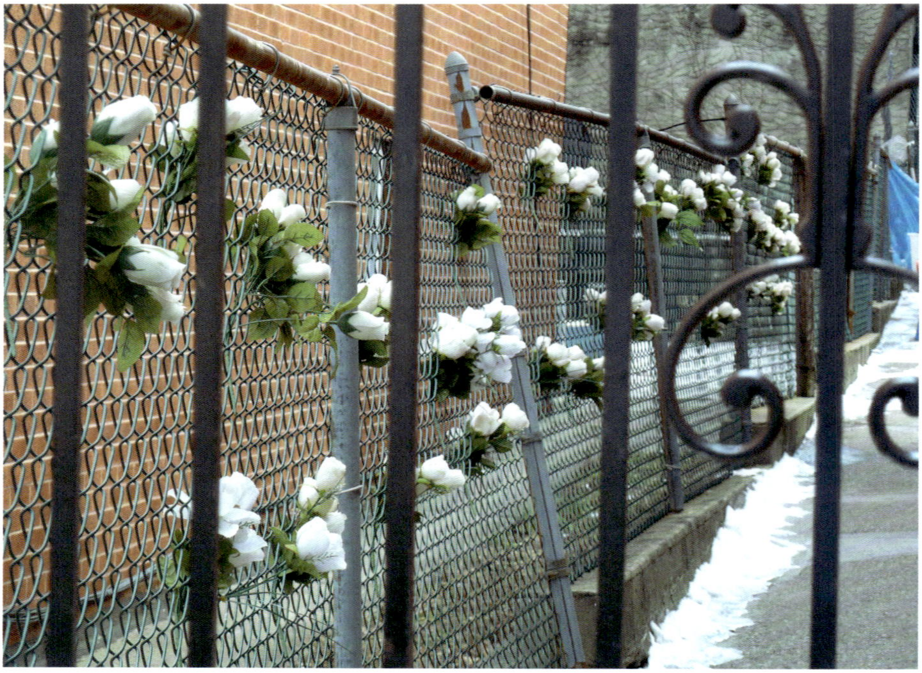

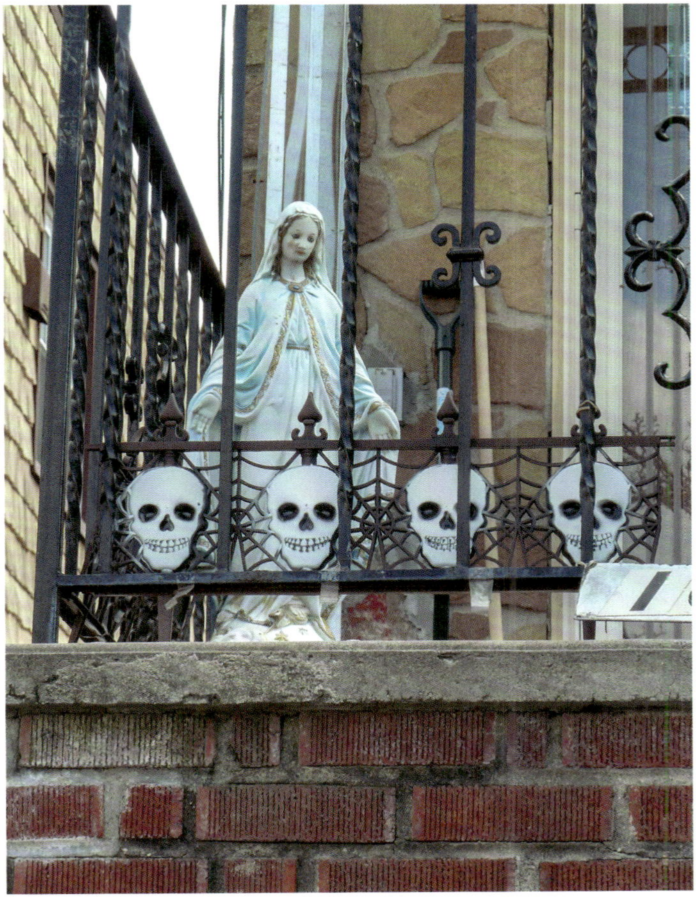

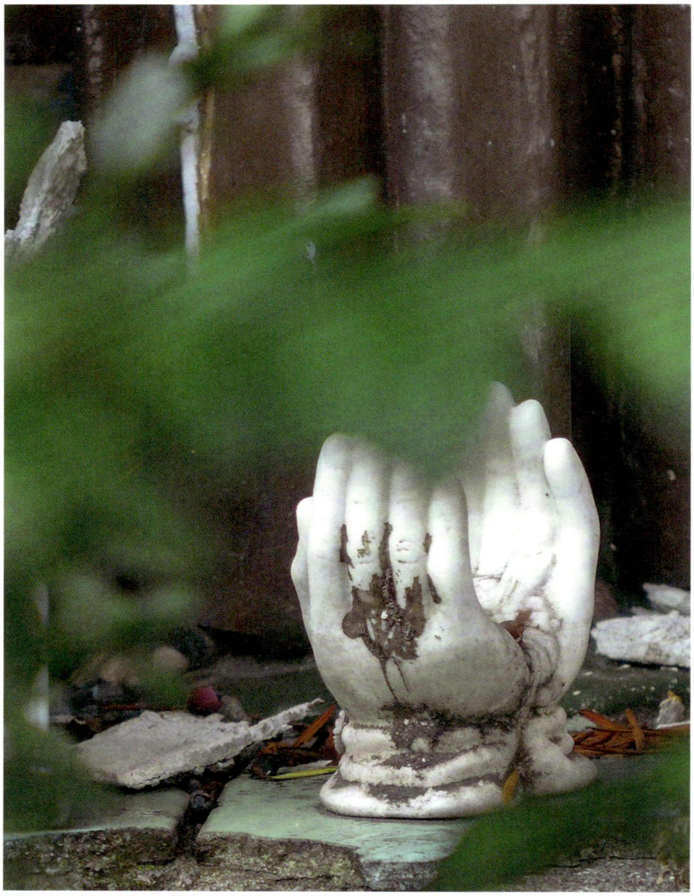

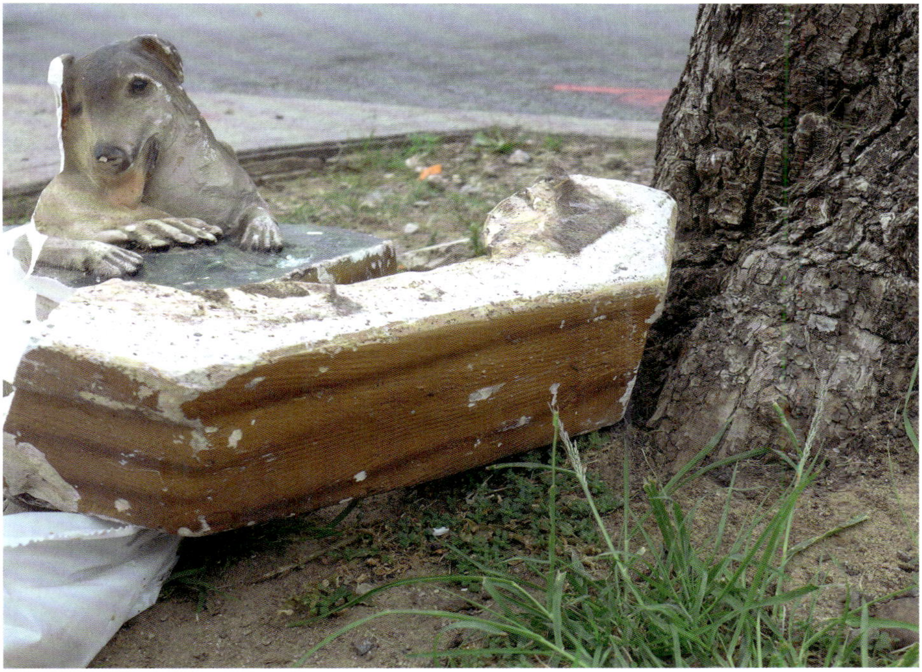

F U

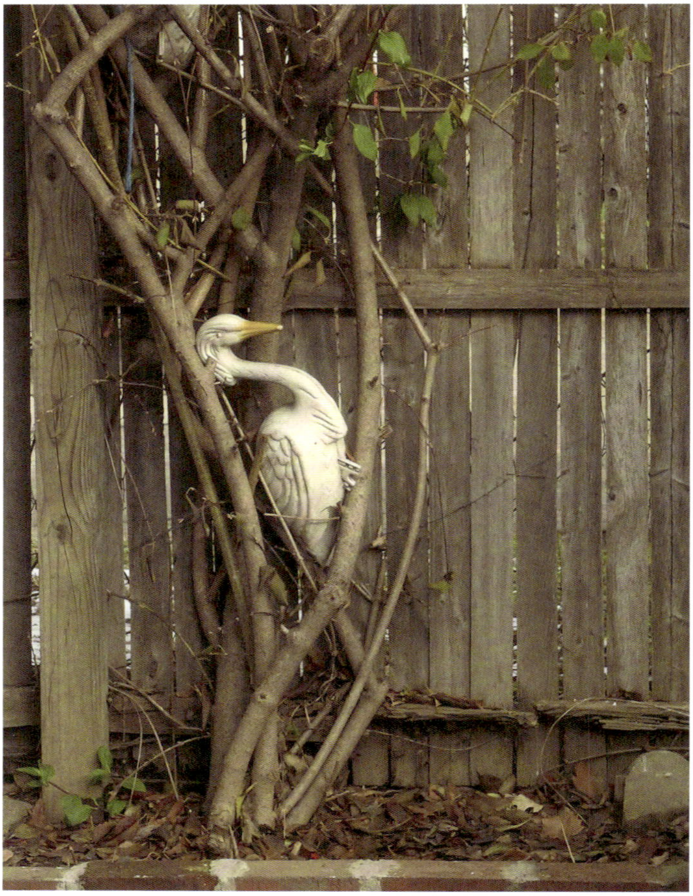

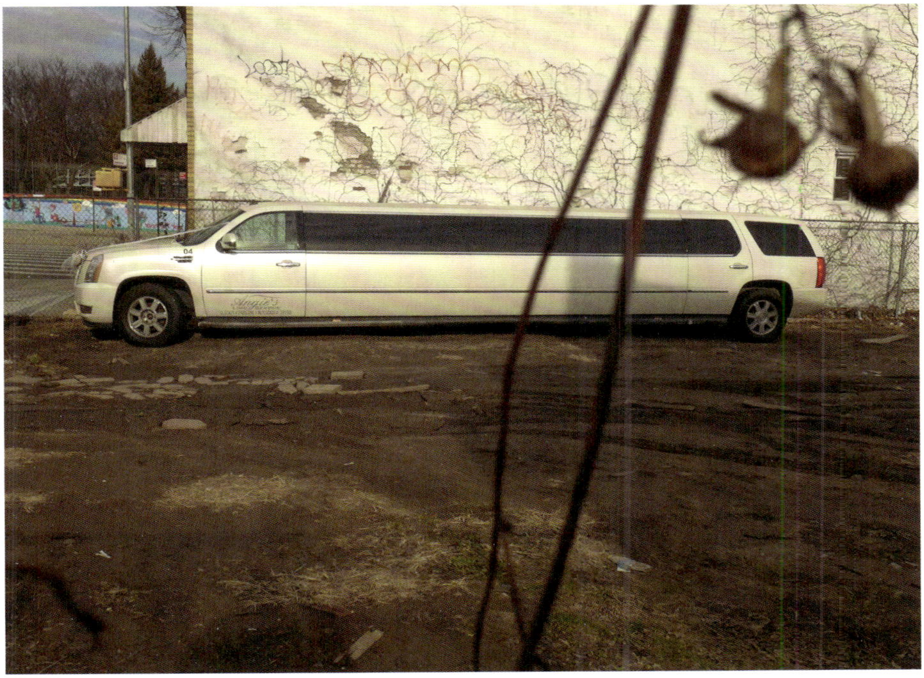

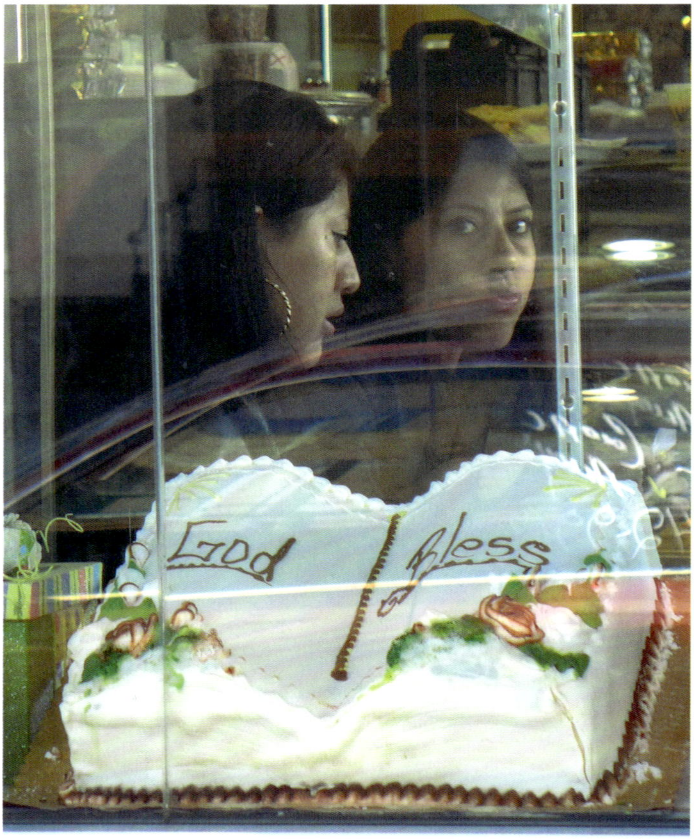
God Bless

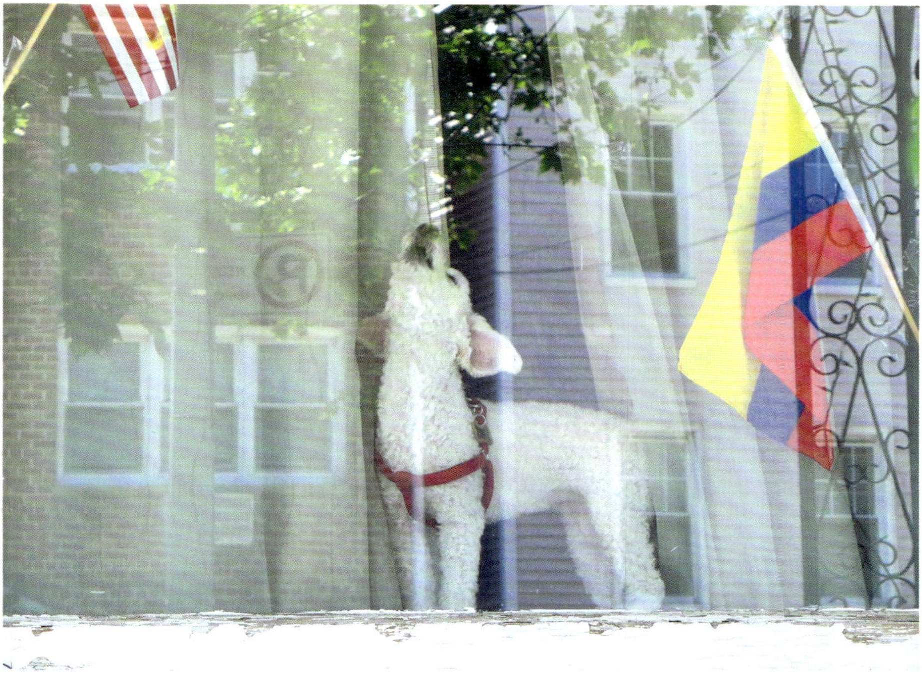

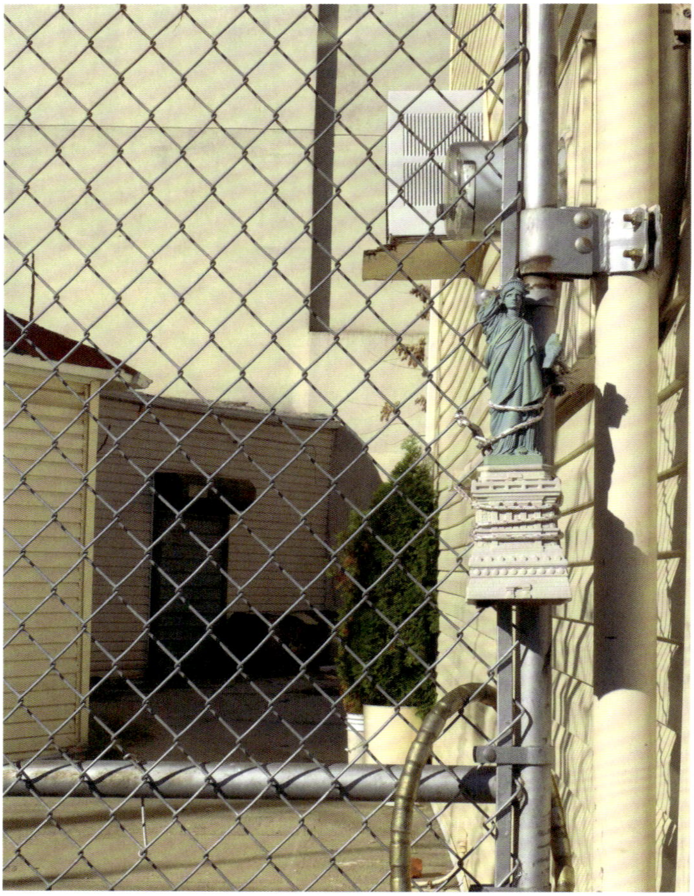

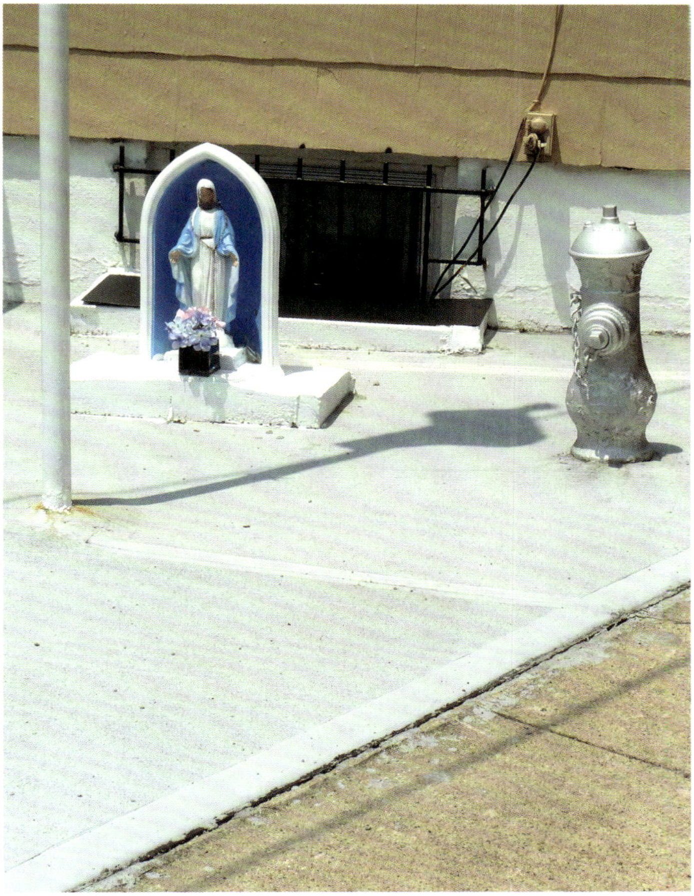

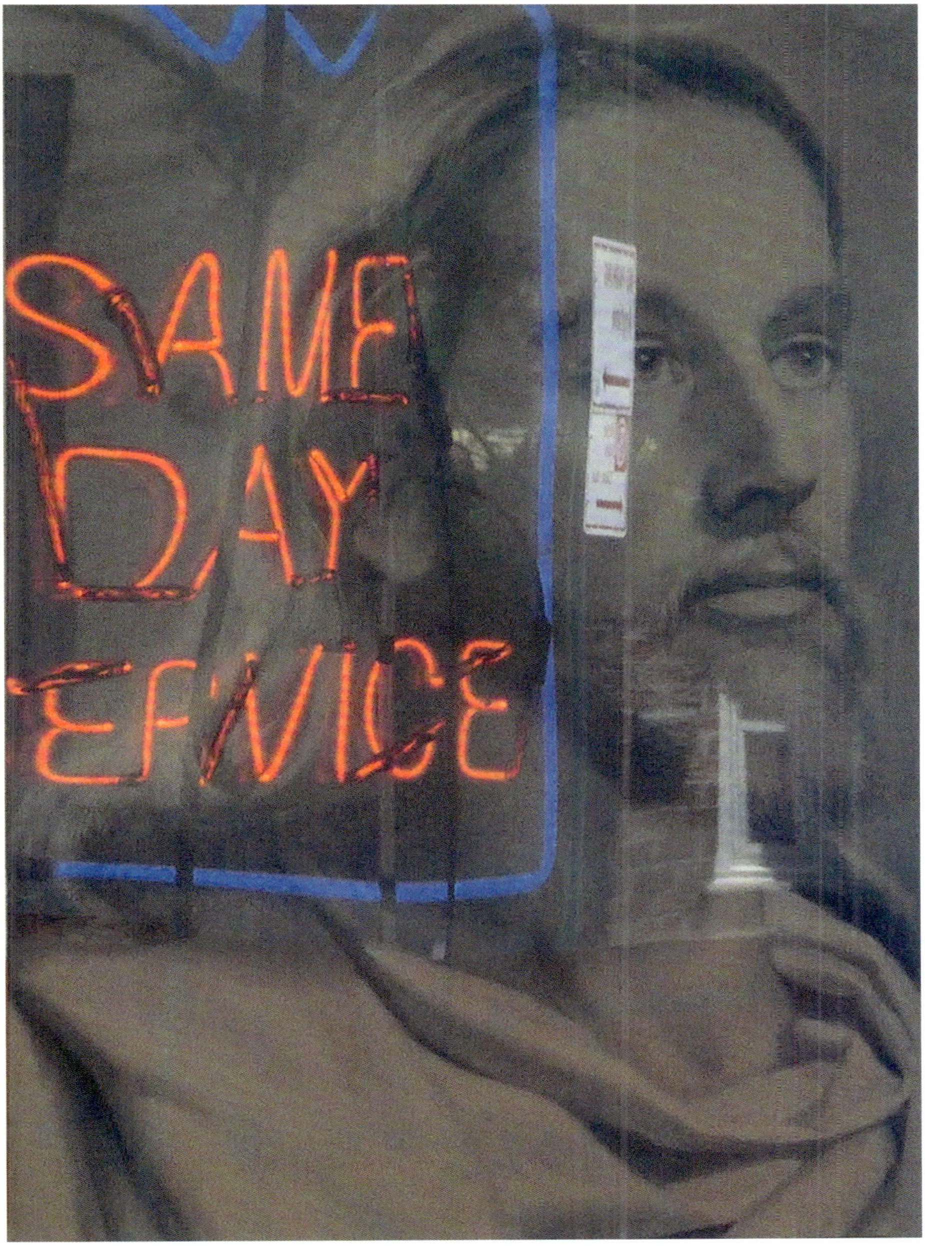
SAME
DAY

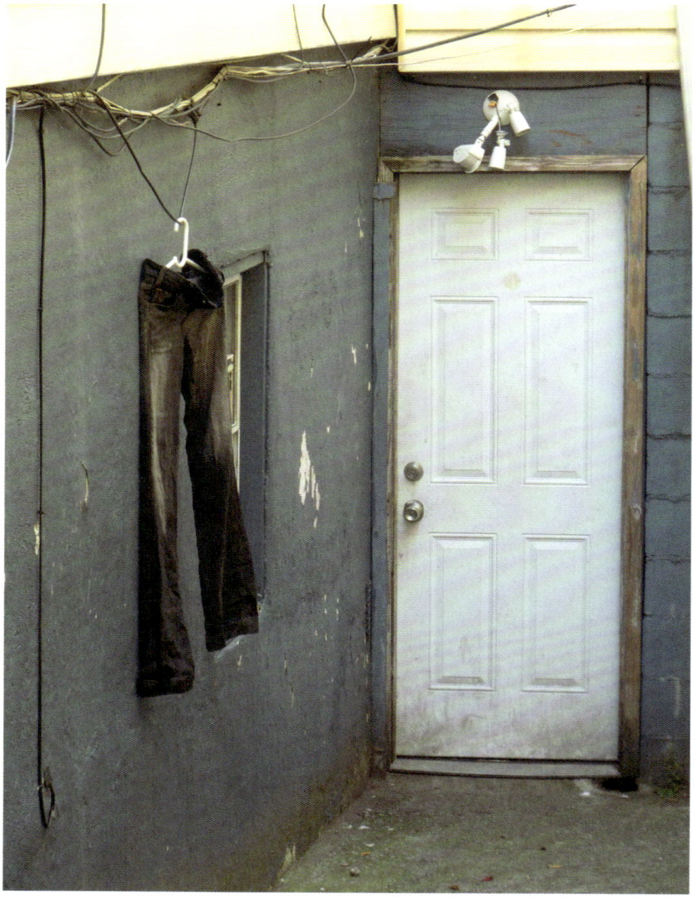

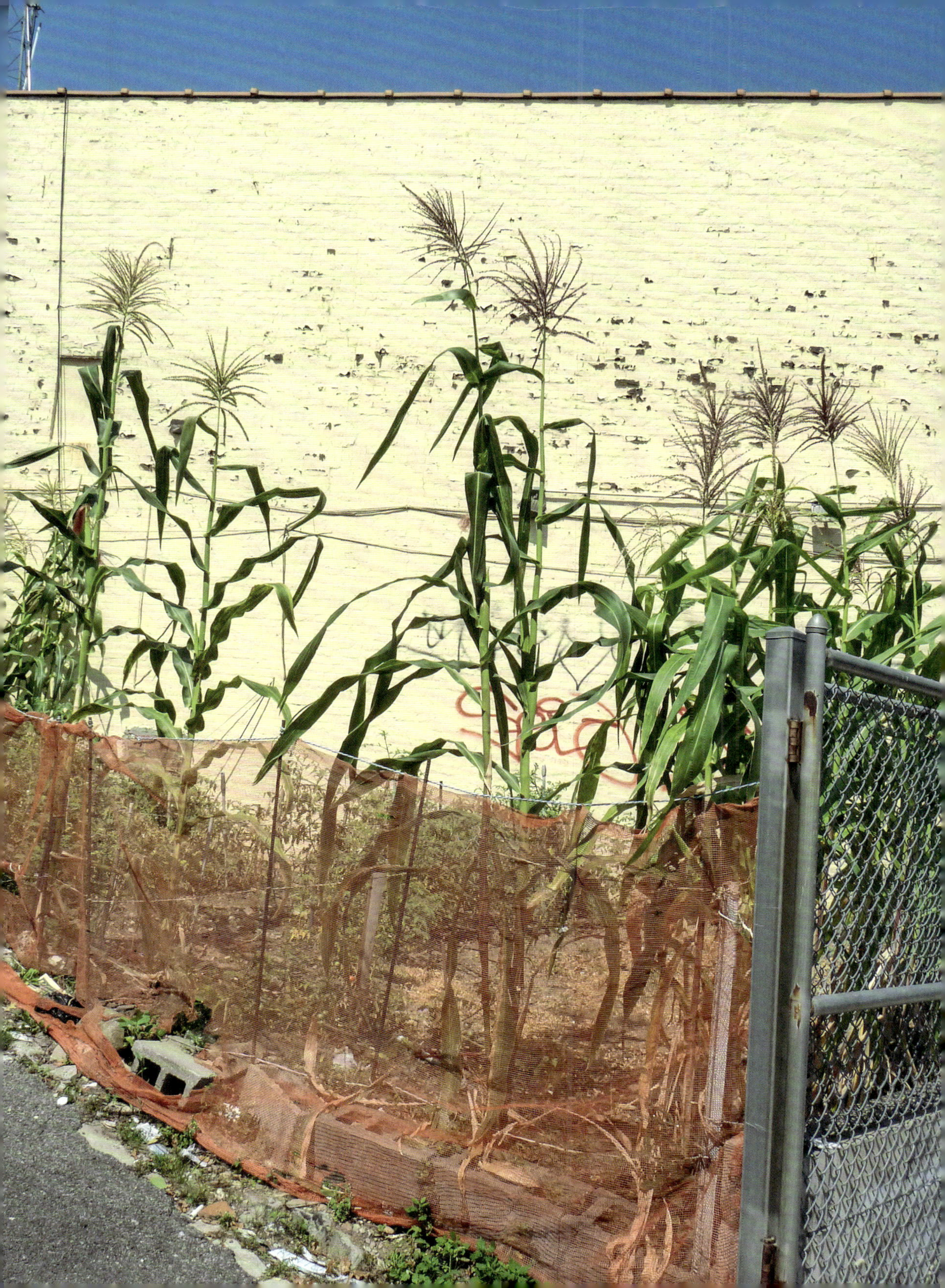

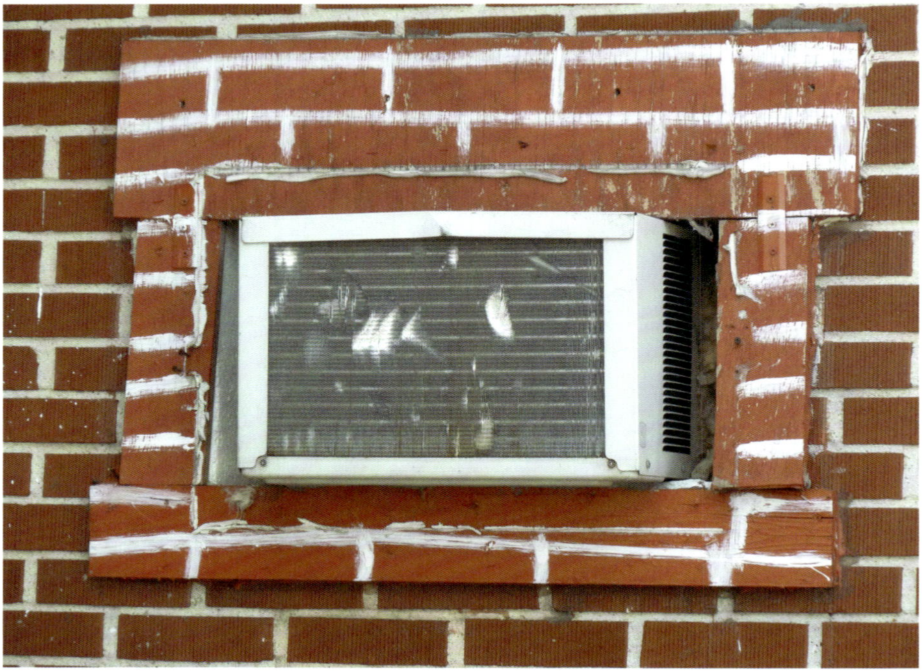

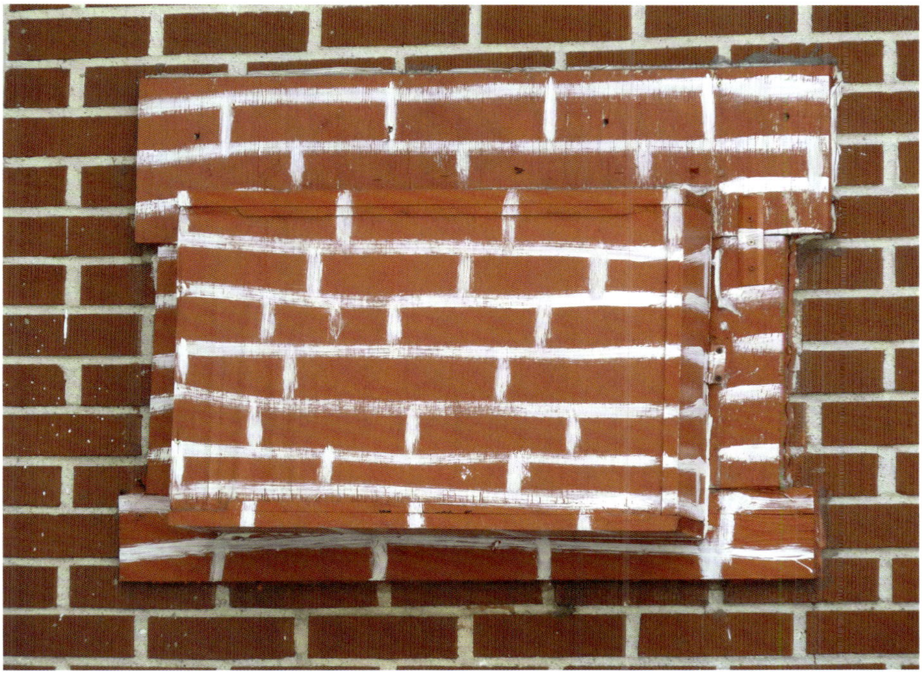

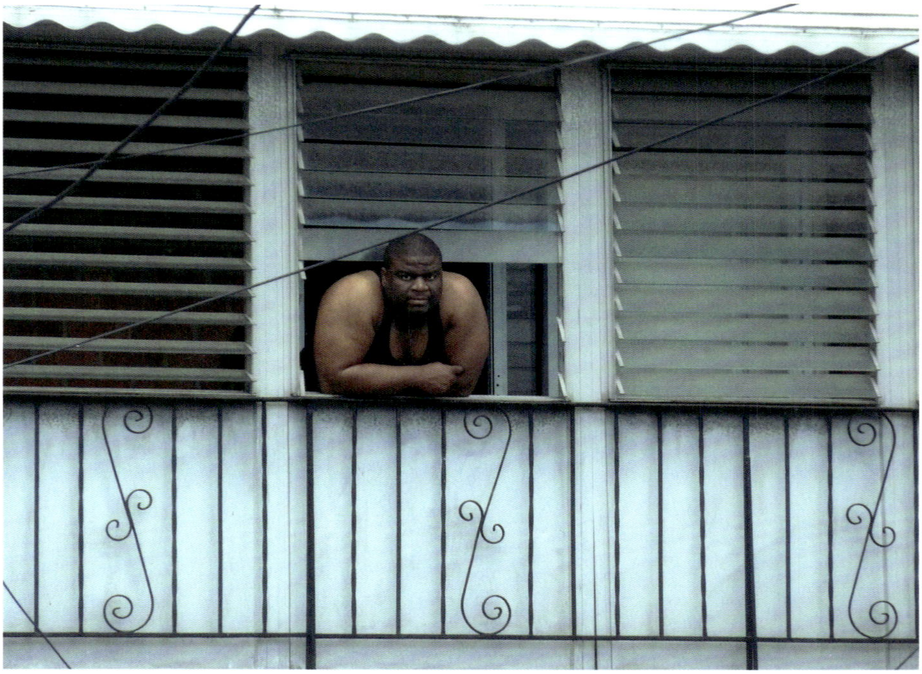

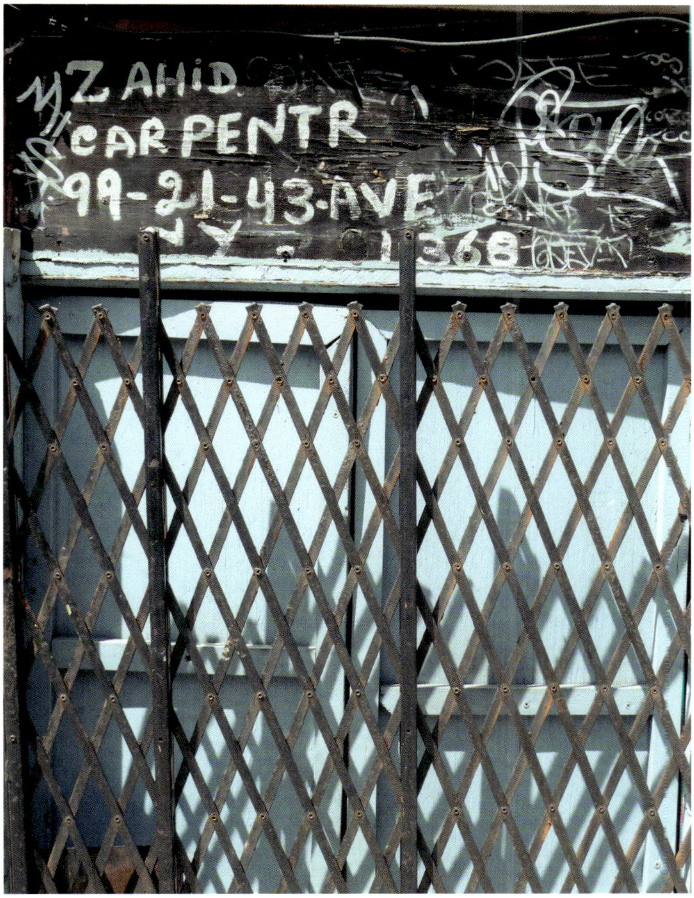
ZAHID
CARPENTR
99-21-43-AVE
NY
1368

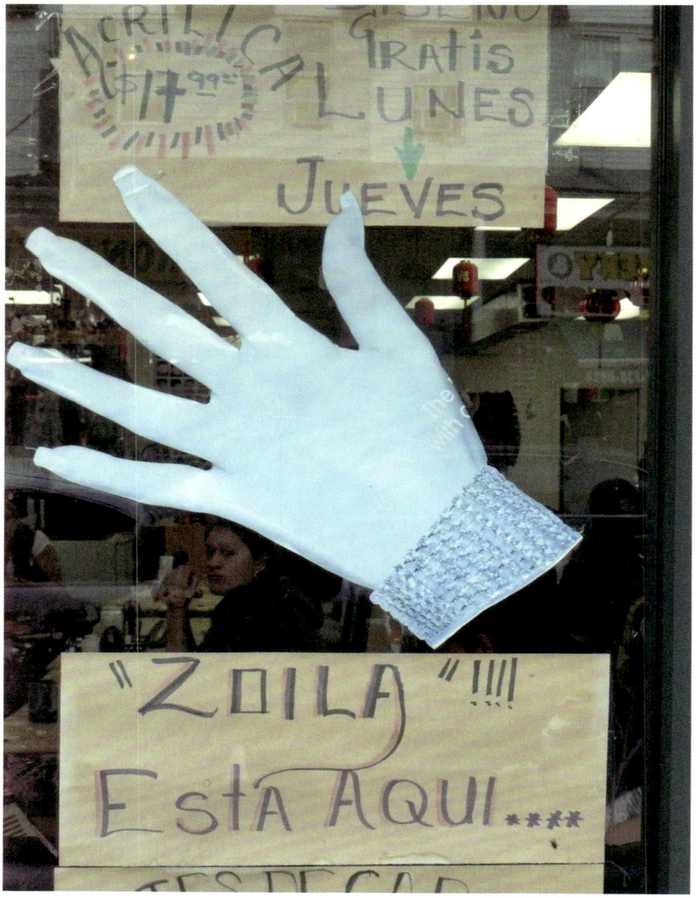
ACRILICA
$17.99
Gratis
LUNES
JUEVES
"ZOILA"!!!!
Esta AQUI....

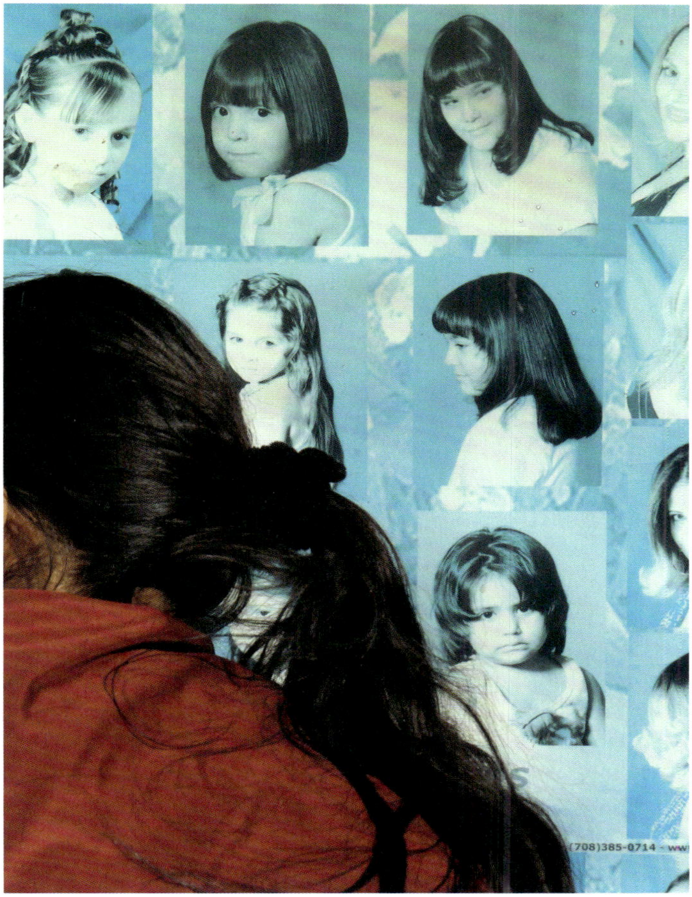
(708)385-0714 -

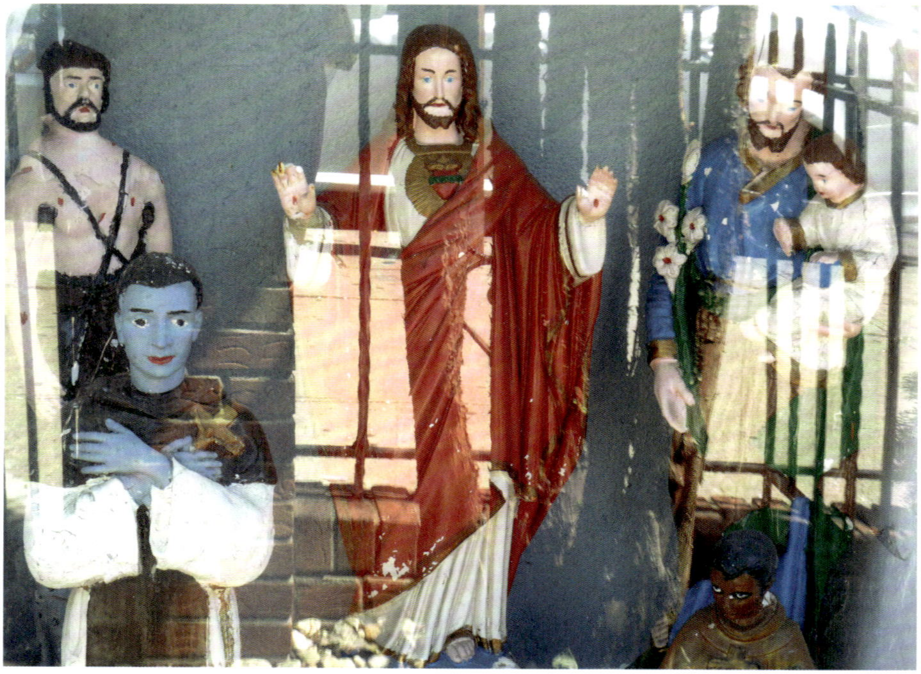

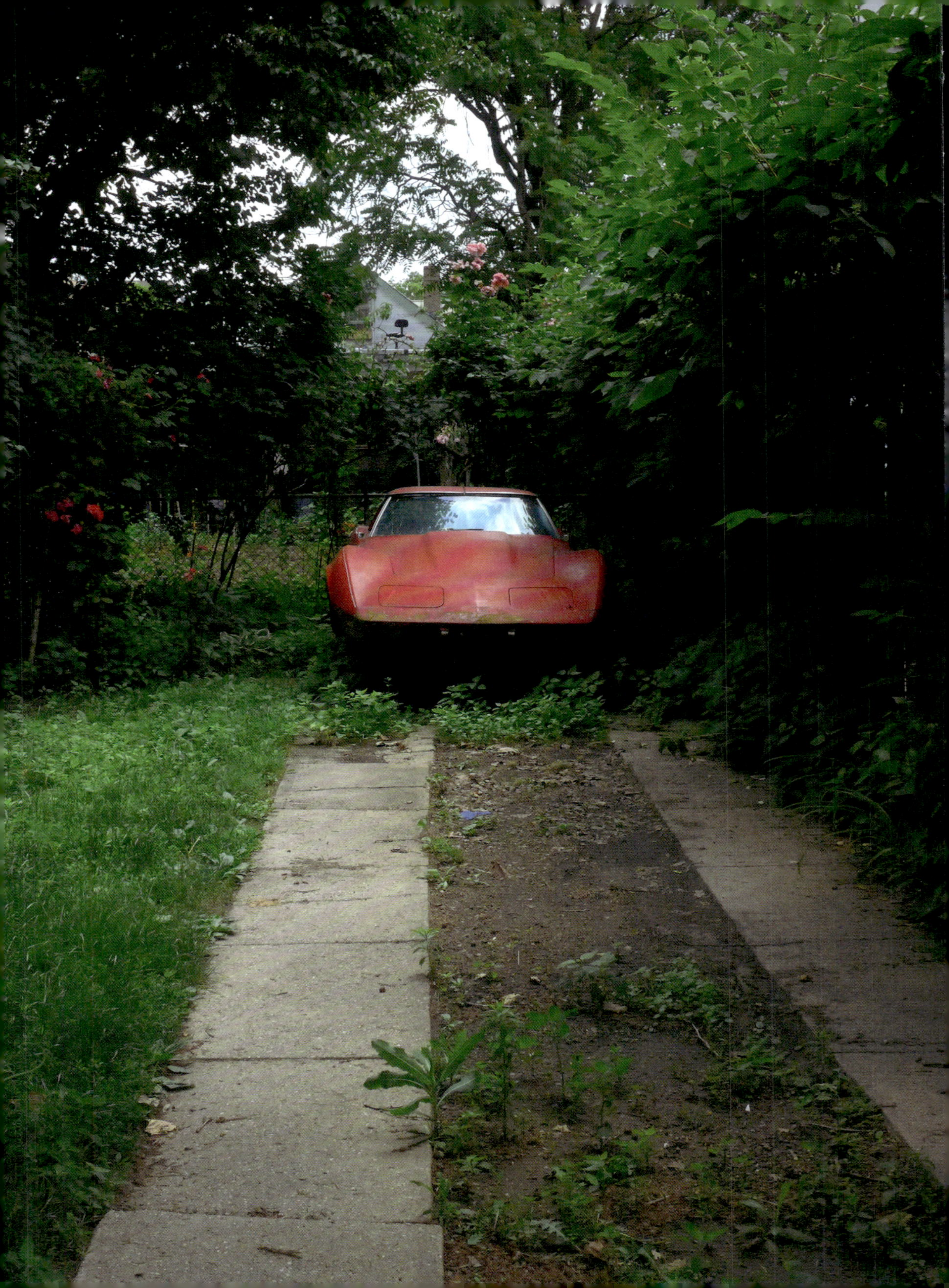

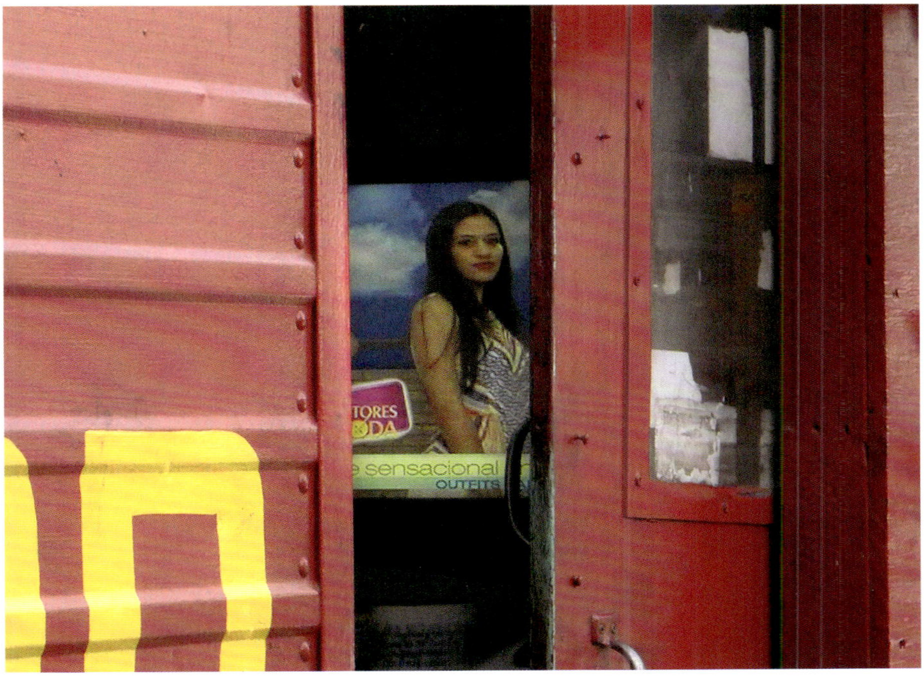
sensacional
OUTFITS

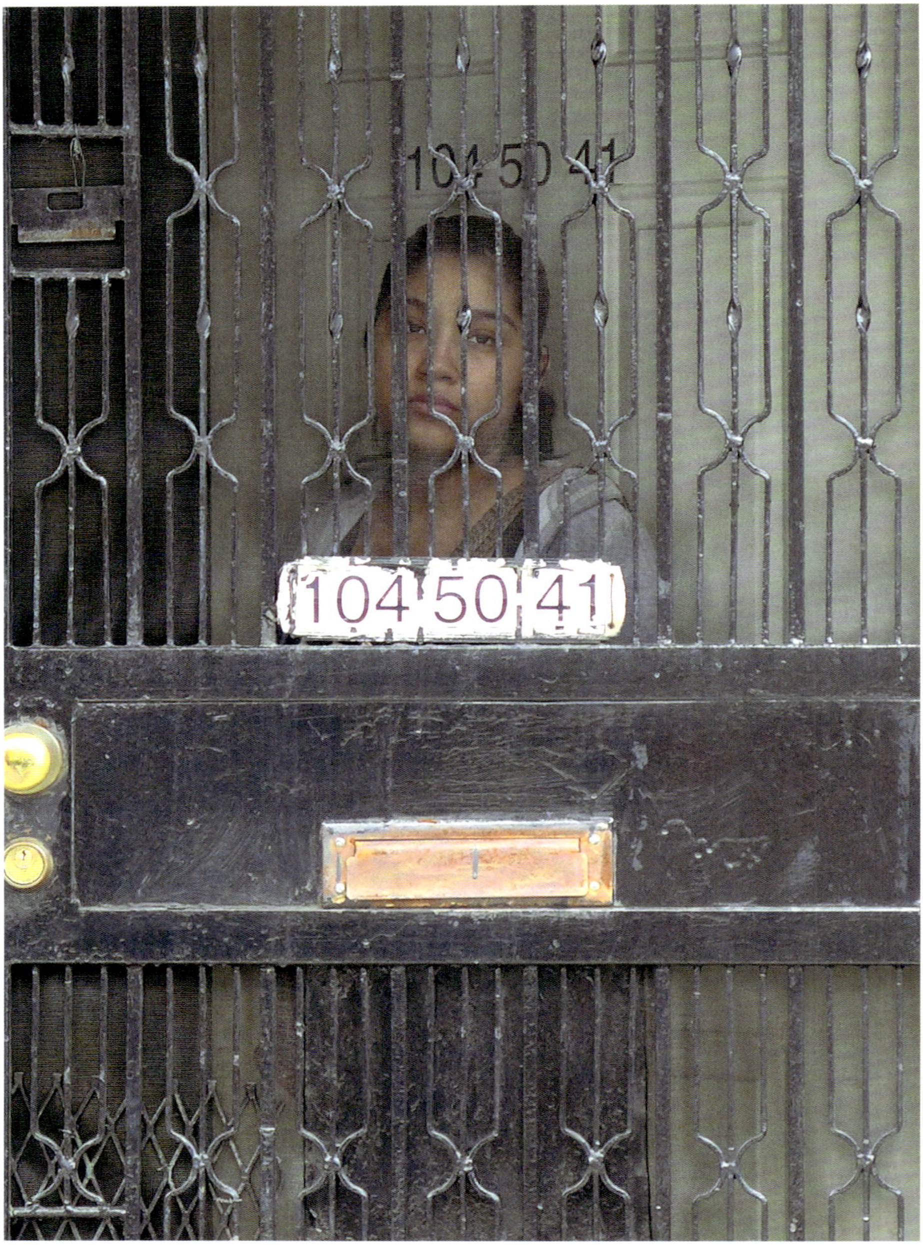
104 50 41
104 50 41

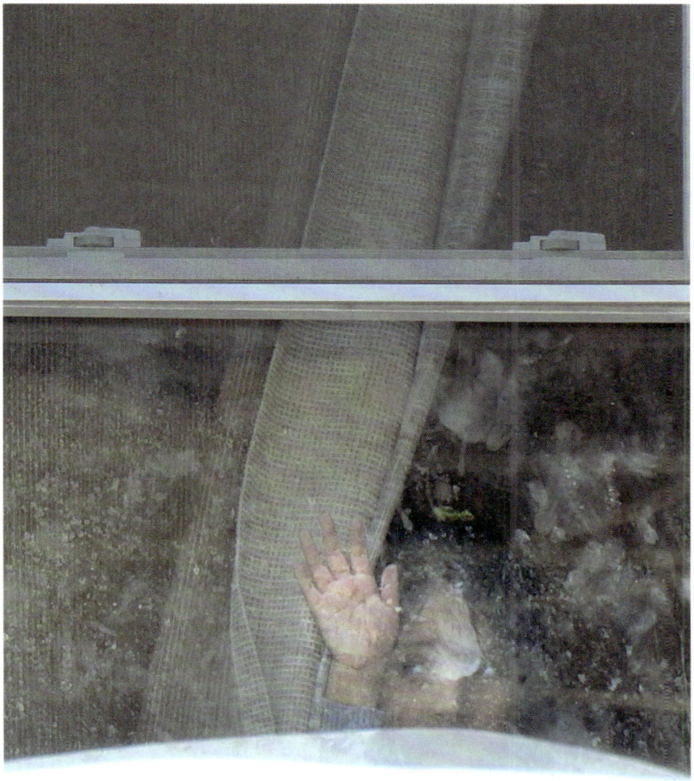

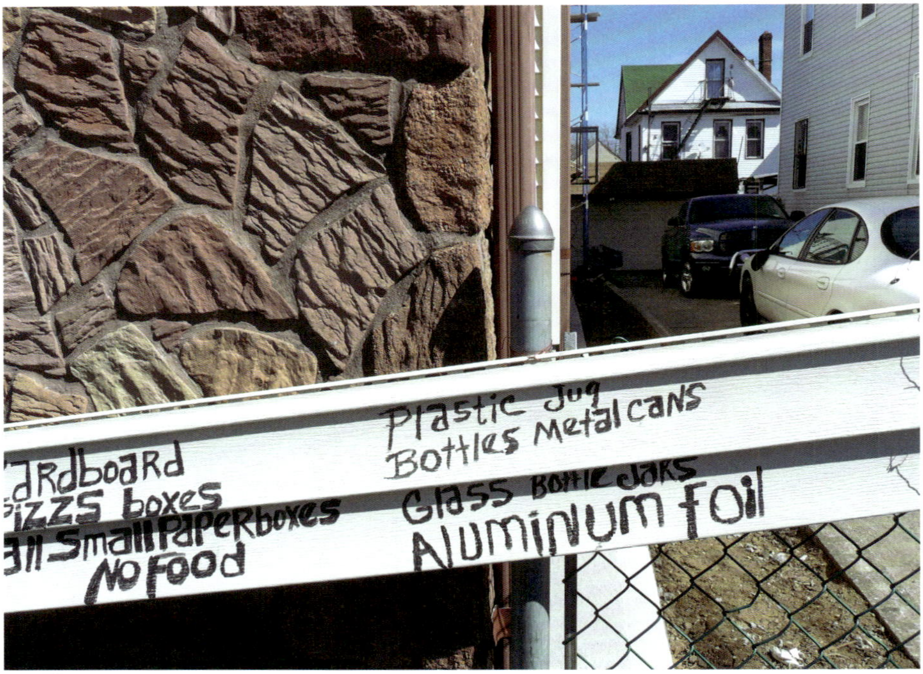
Plastic Jug
Bottles Metal cans
Glass Bottle Jars
Aluminum Foil
boxes
Small paper boxes
No Food

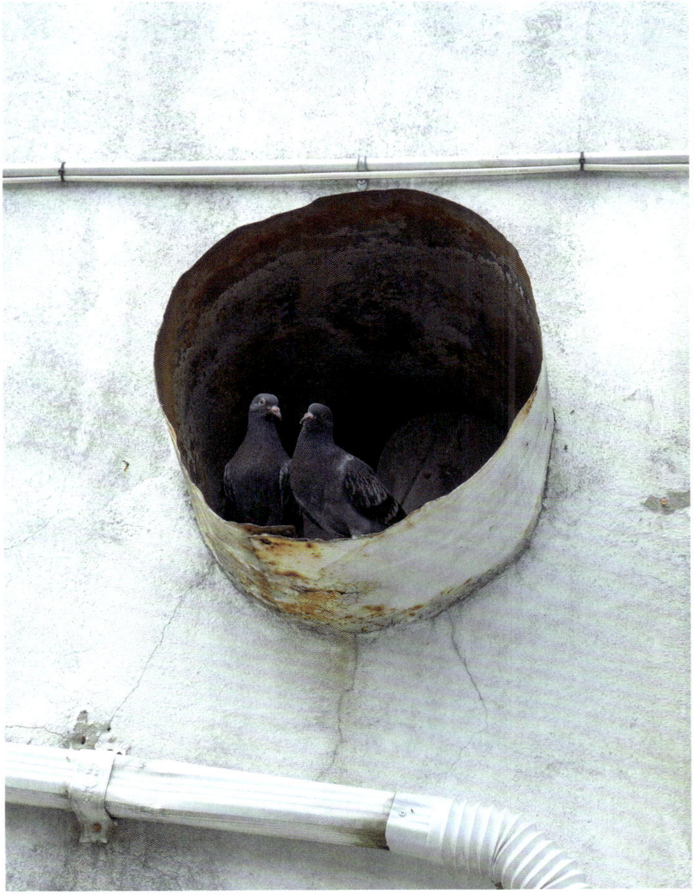

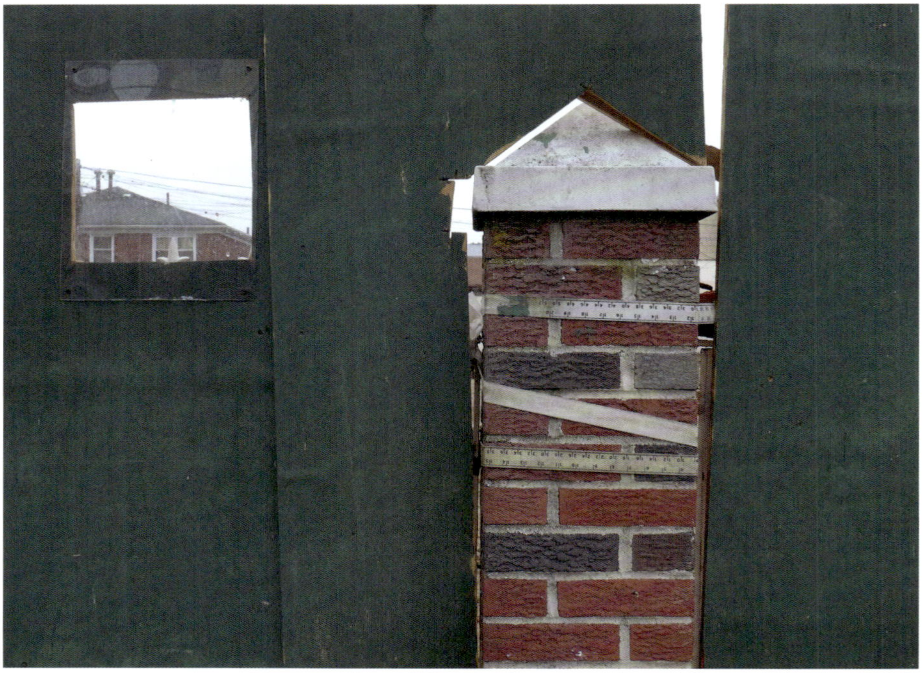

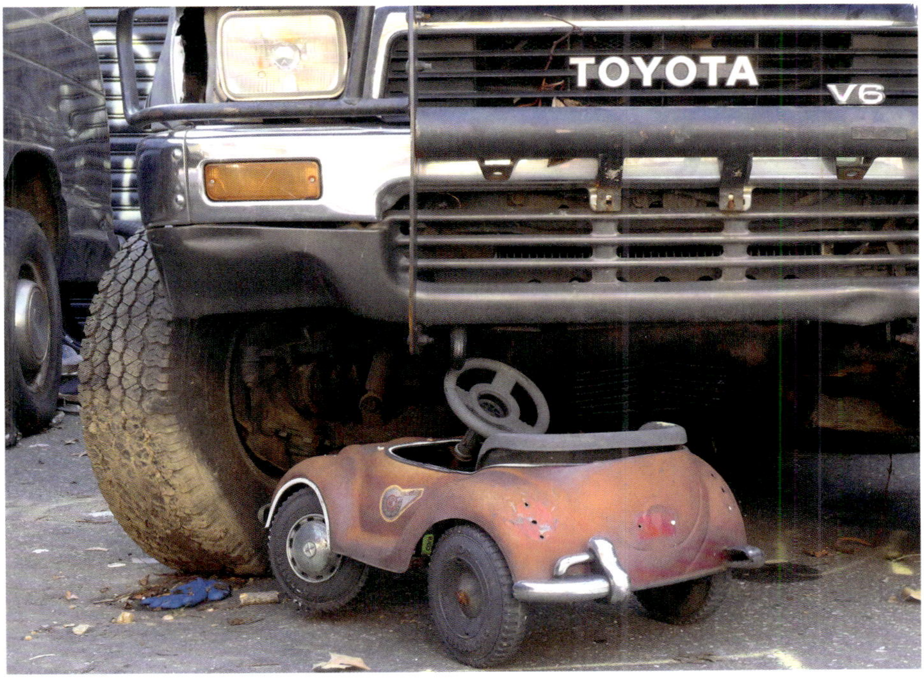
TOYOTA
V6

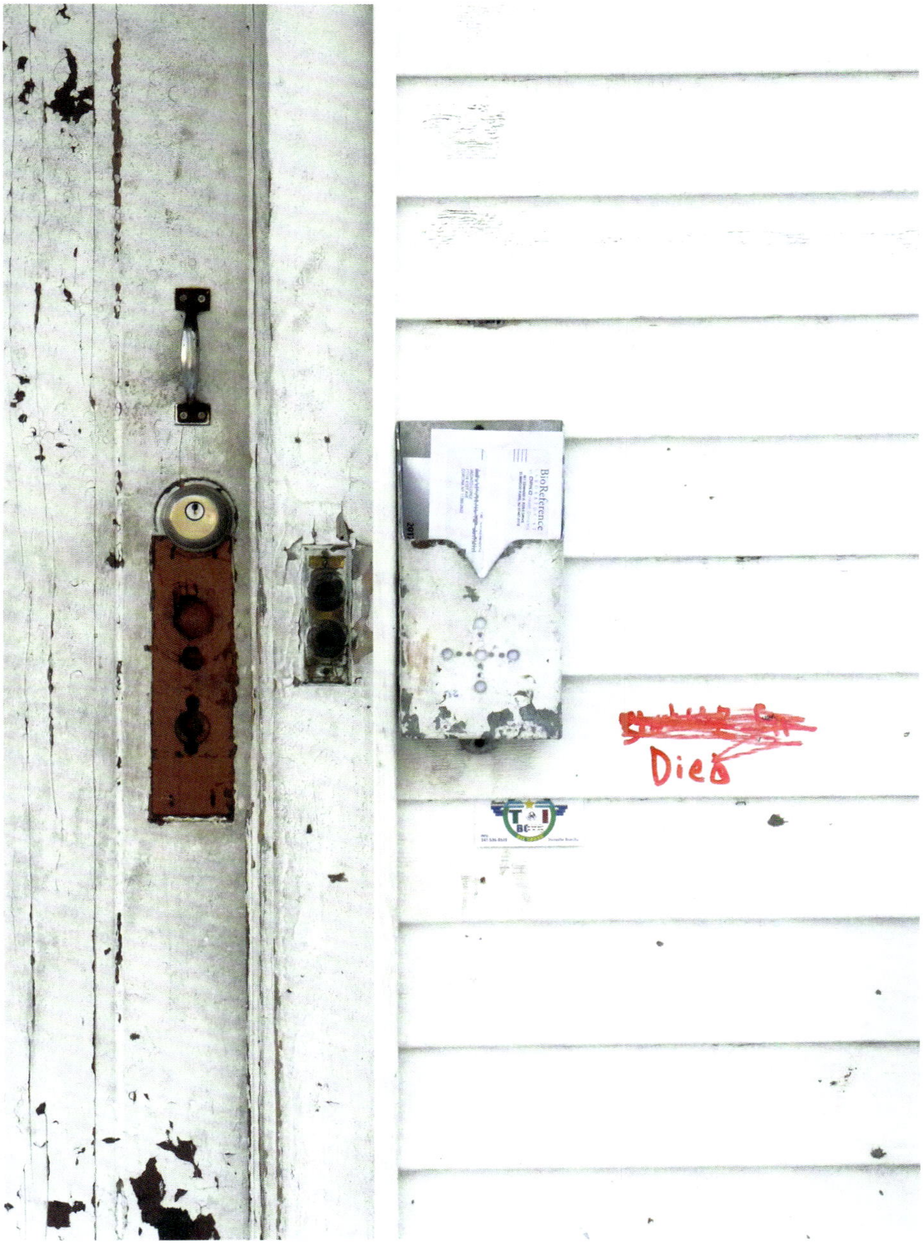
Died

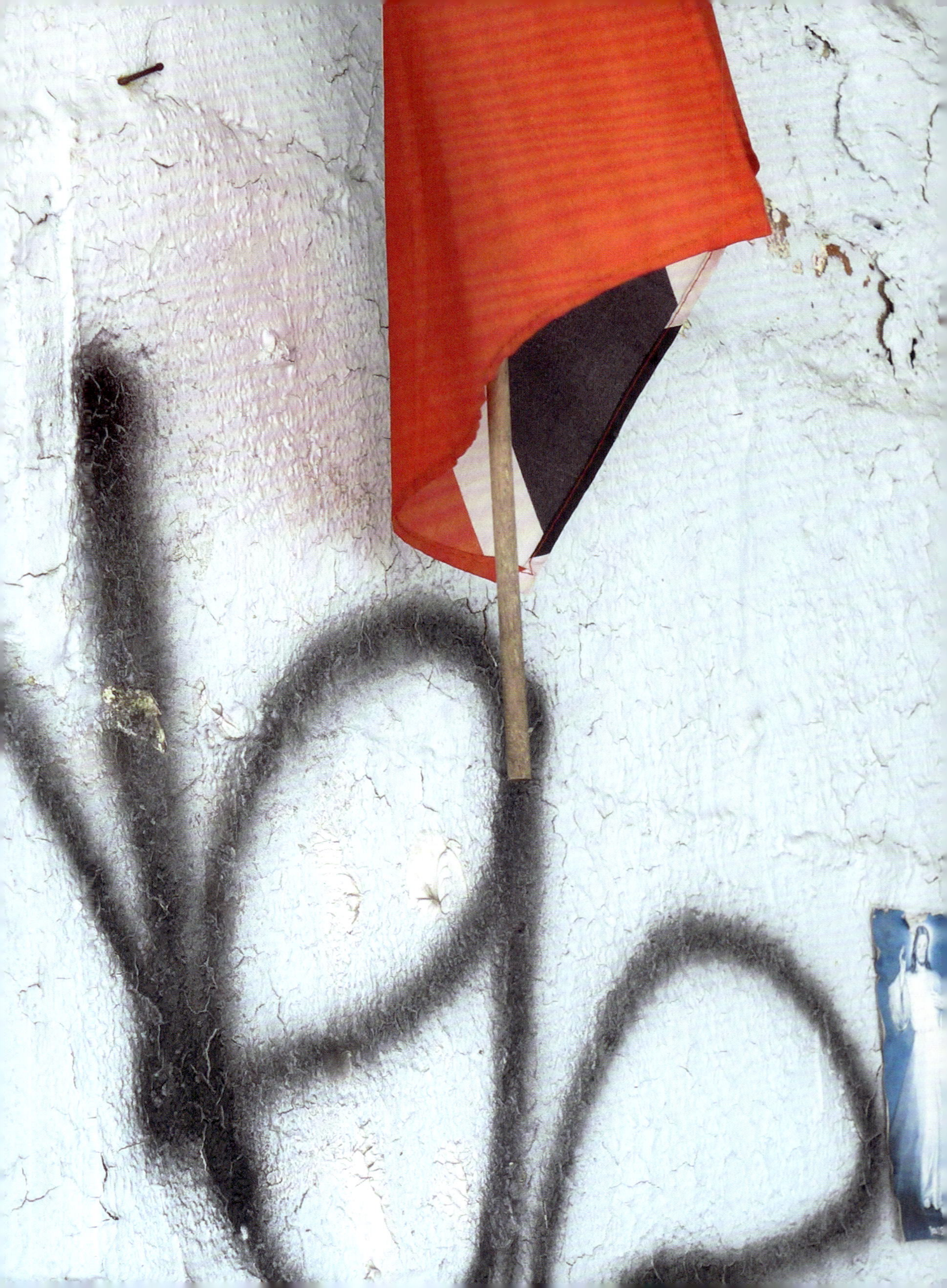

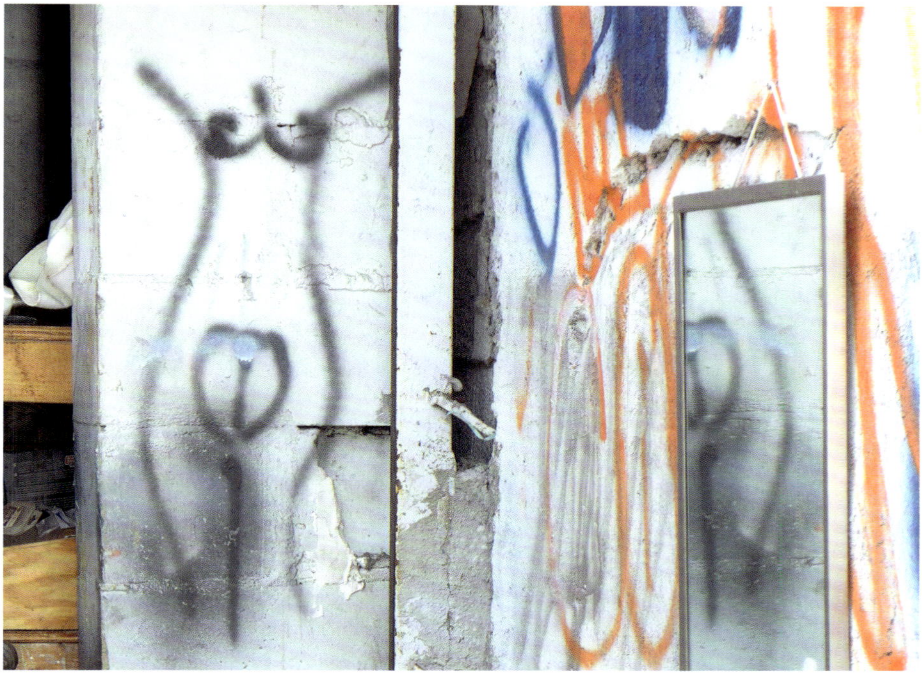

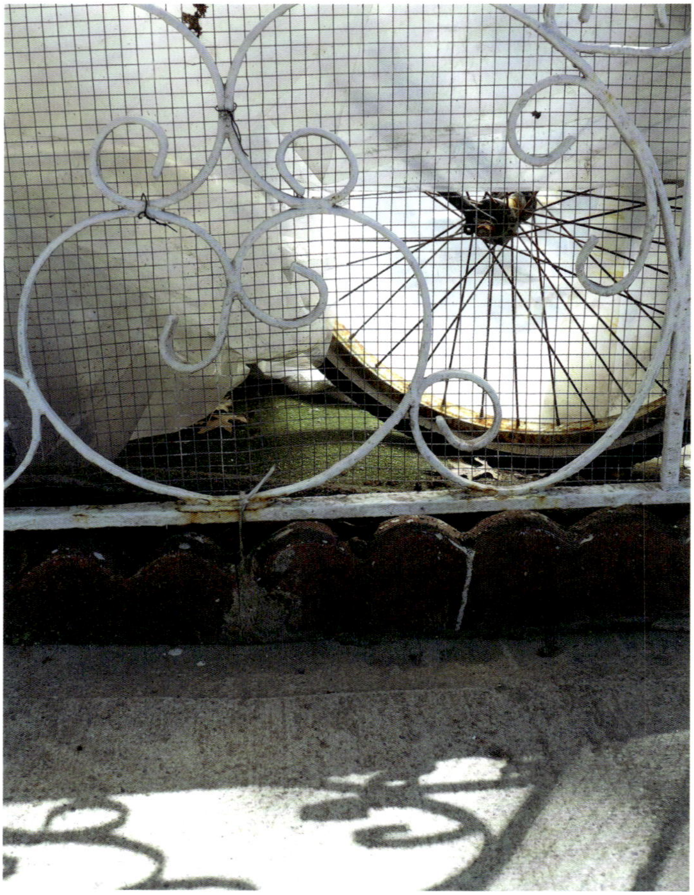

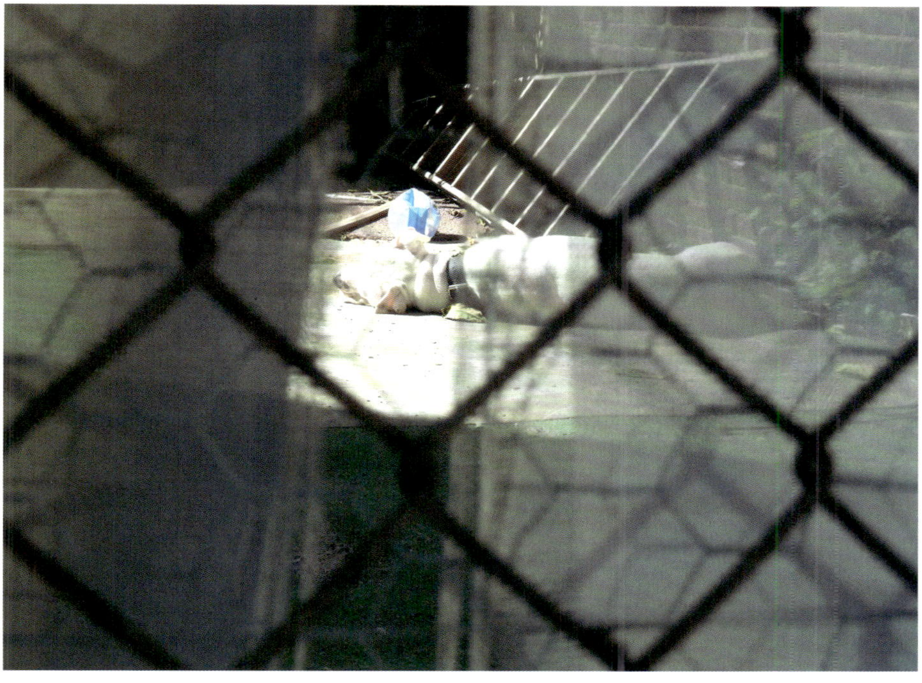

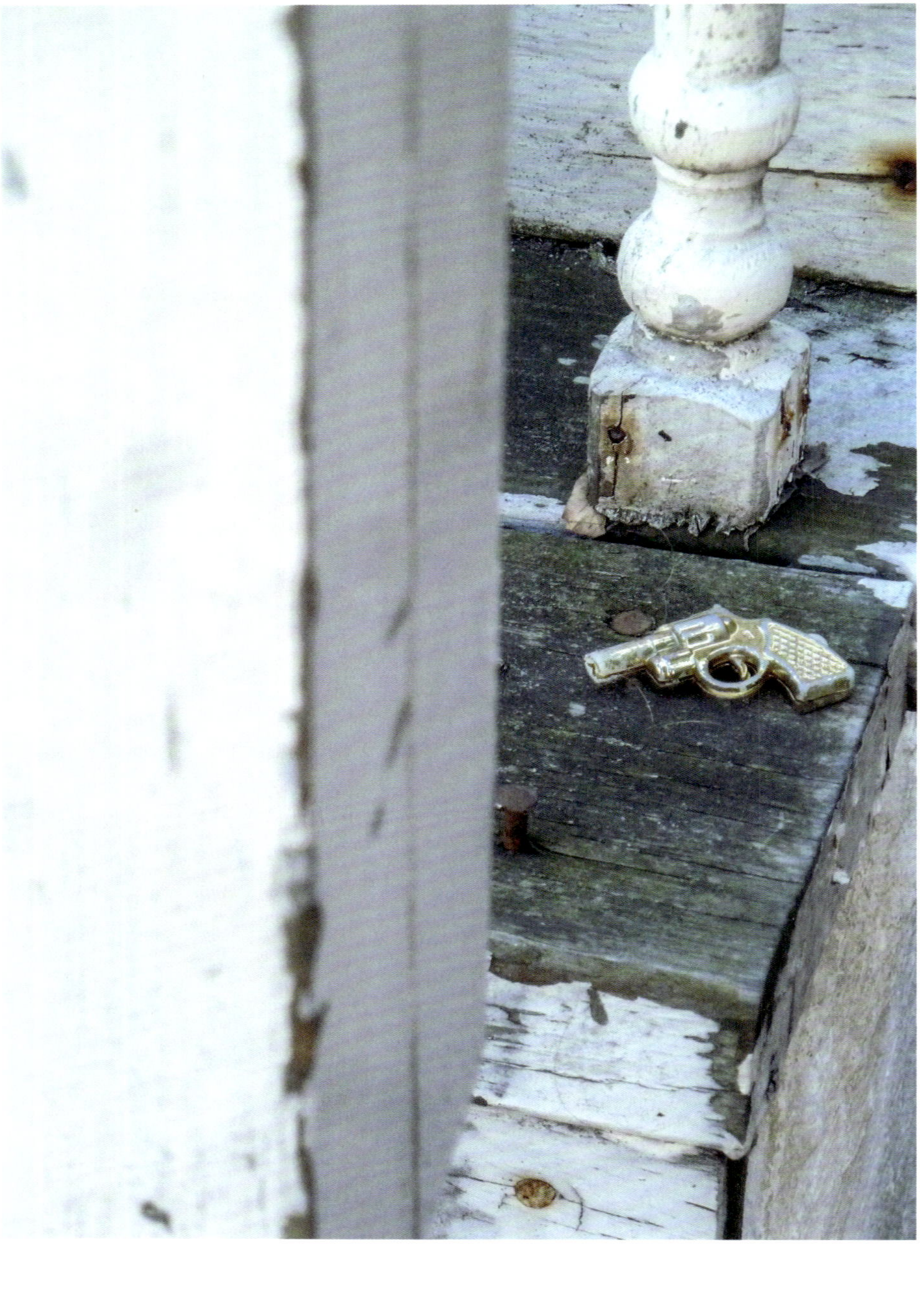

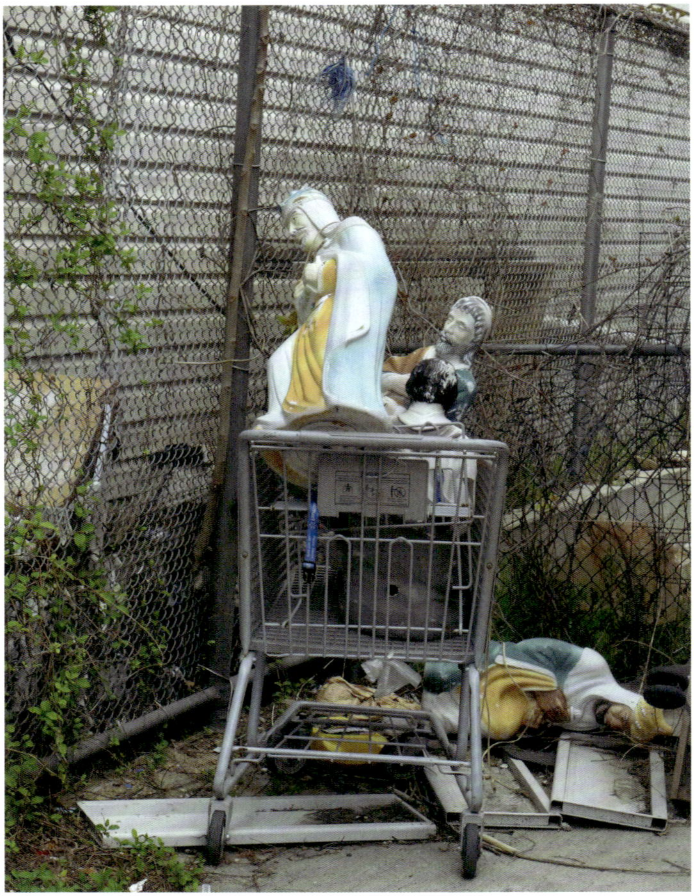

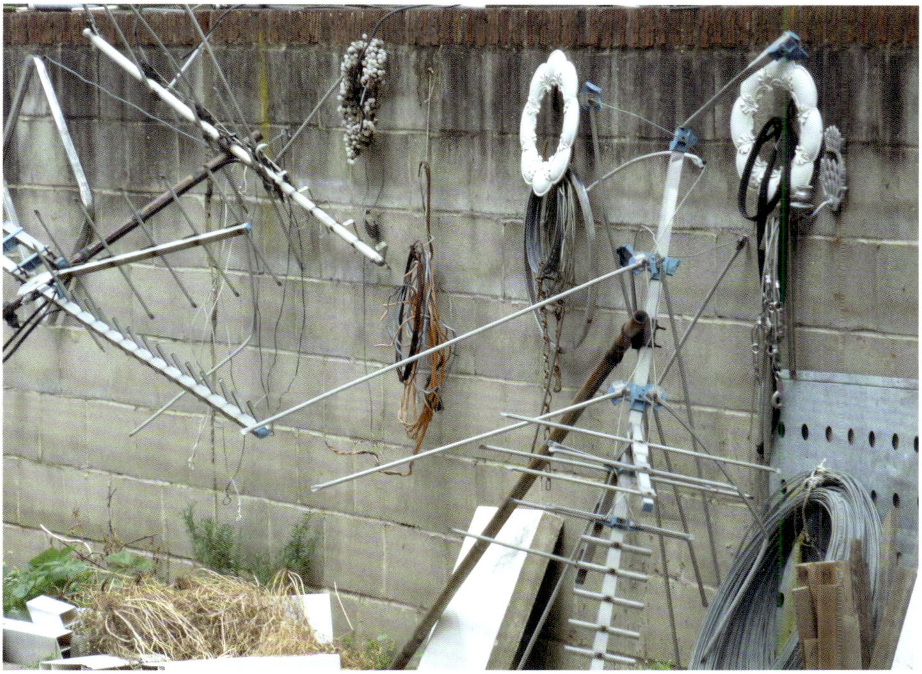

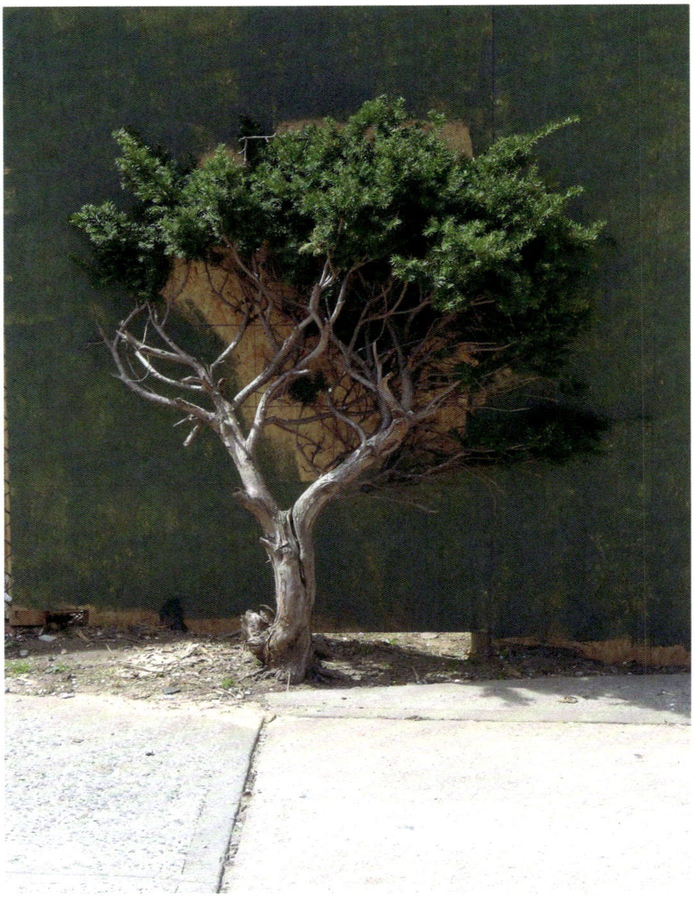

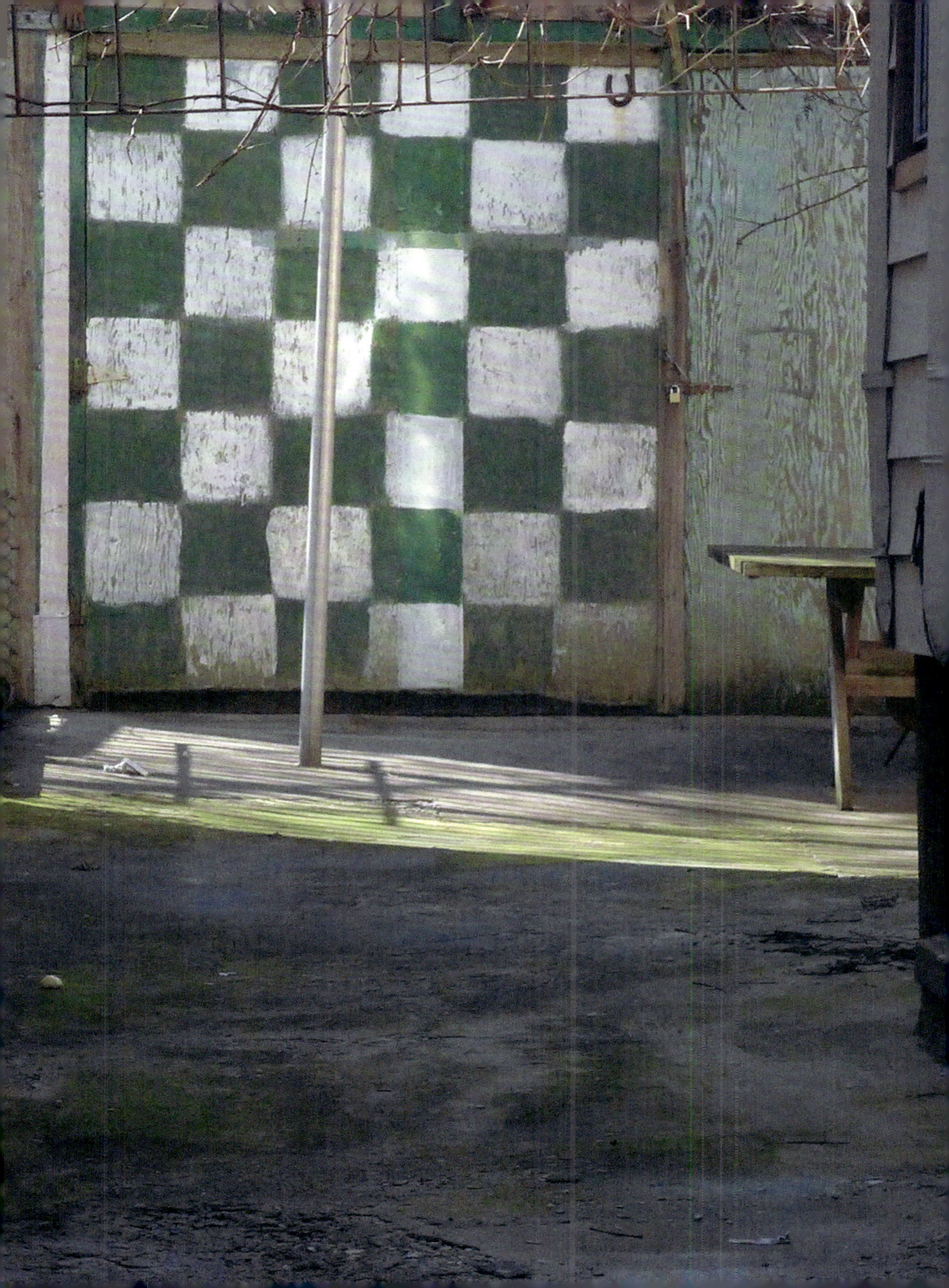

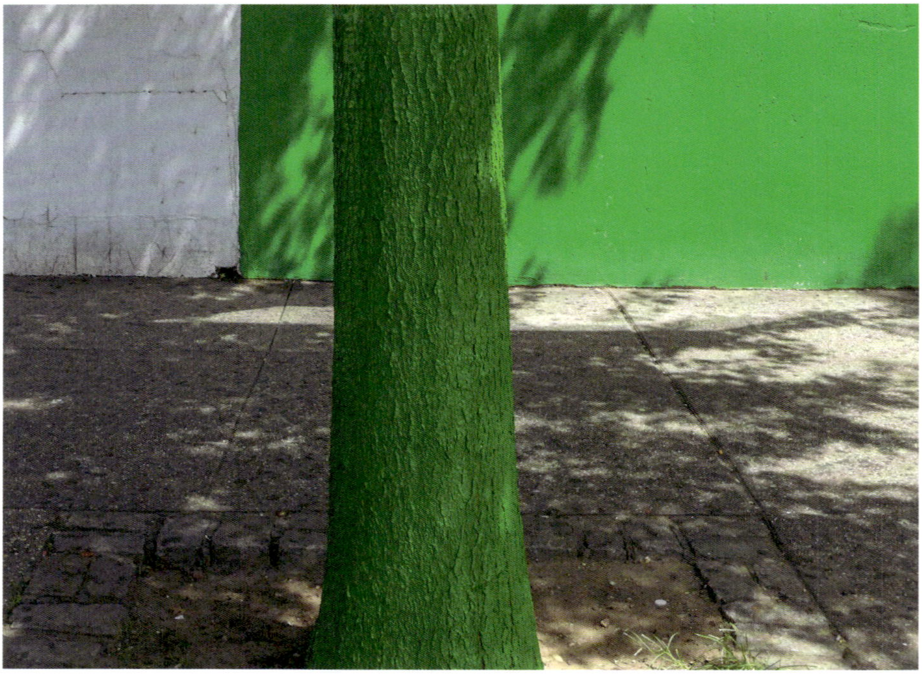

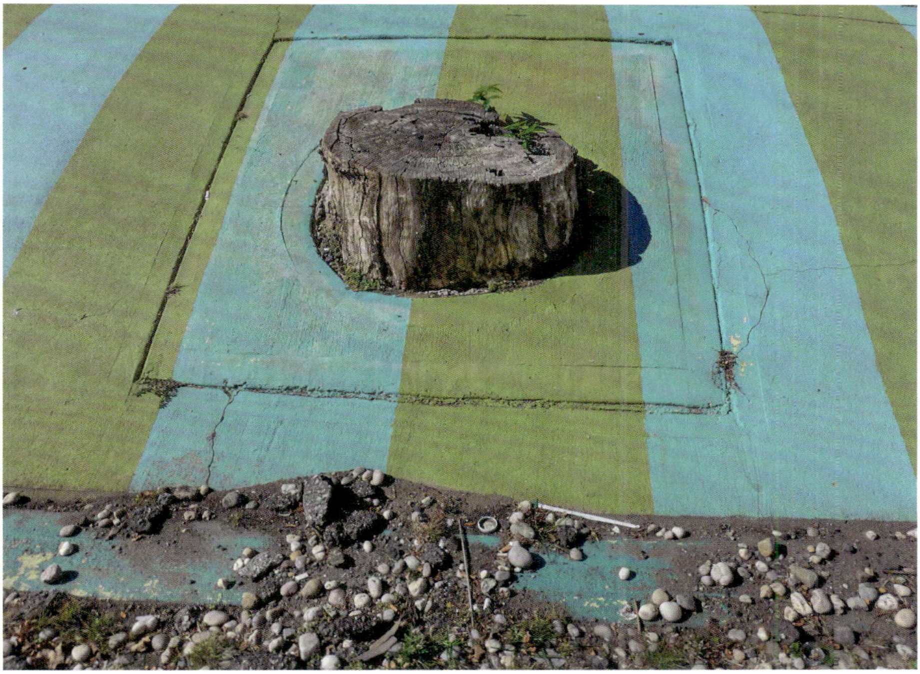

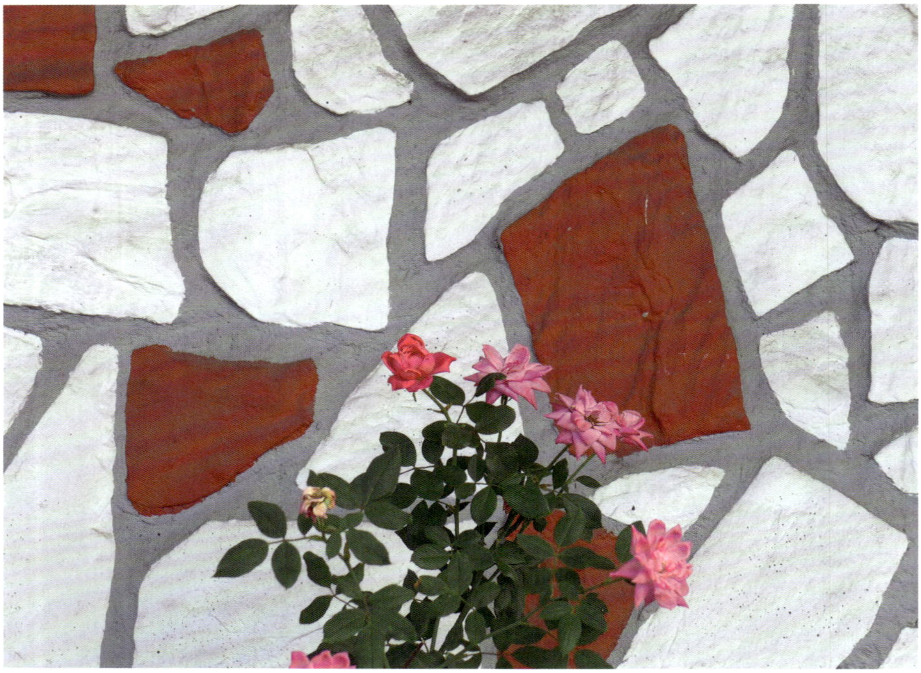

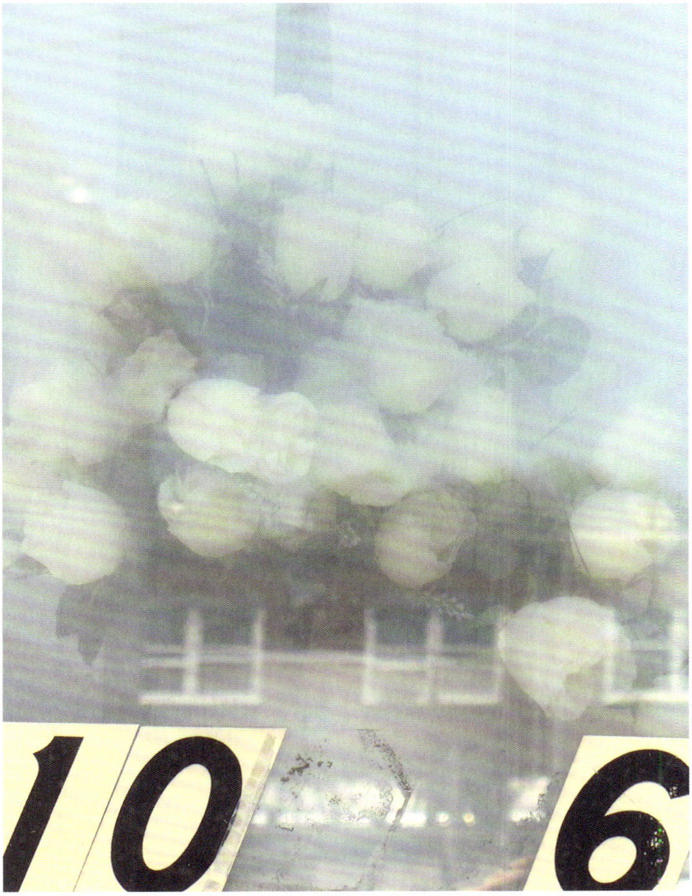
10
6

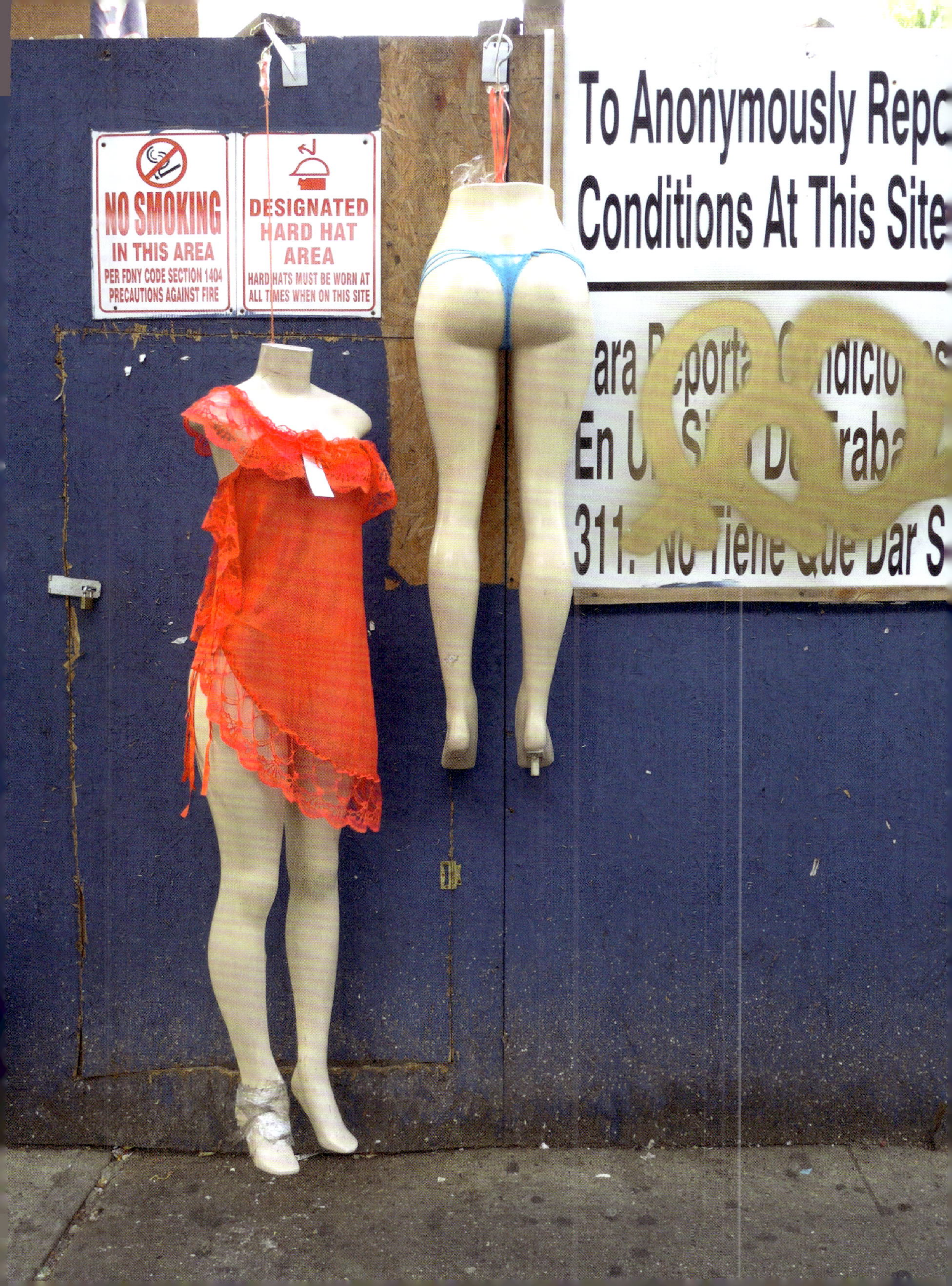
NO SMOKING
IN THIS AREA
PER FDNY CODE SECTION 1404
PRECAUTIONS AGAINST FIRE
DESIGNATED
HARD HAT
AREA
HARD HATS MUST BE WORN AT
ALL TIMES WHEN ON THIS SITE
Conditions At This Site

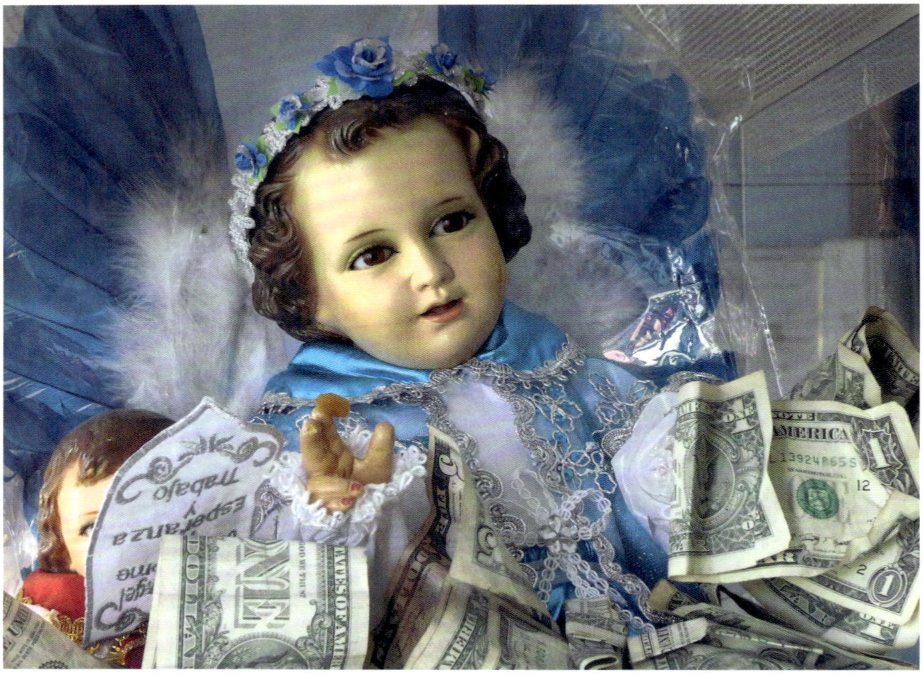
Trabajo
y
Esperanza a
AMERICA

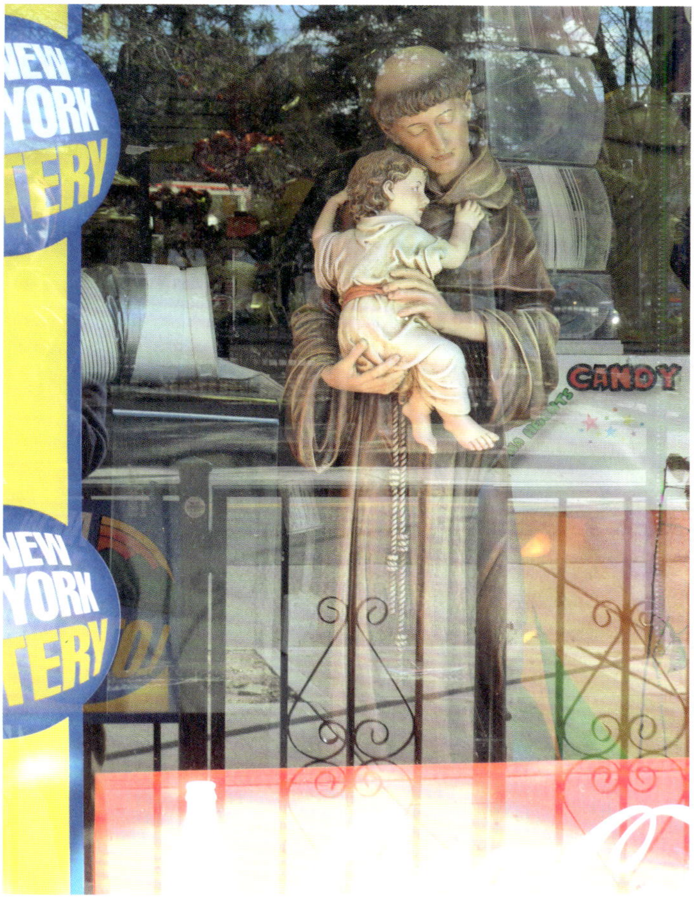
NEW
YORK
TERY
CANDY
NEW
YORK
TERY

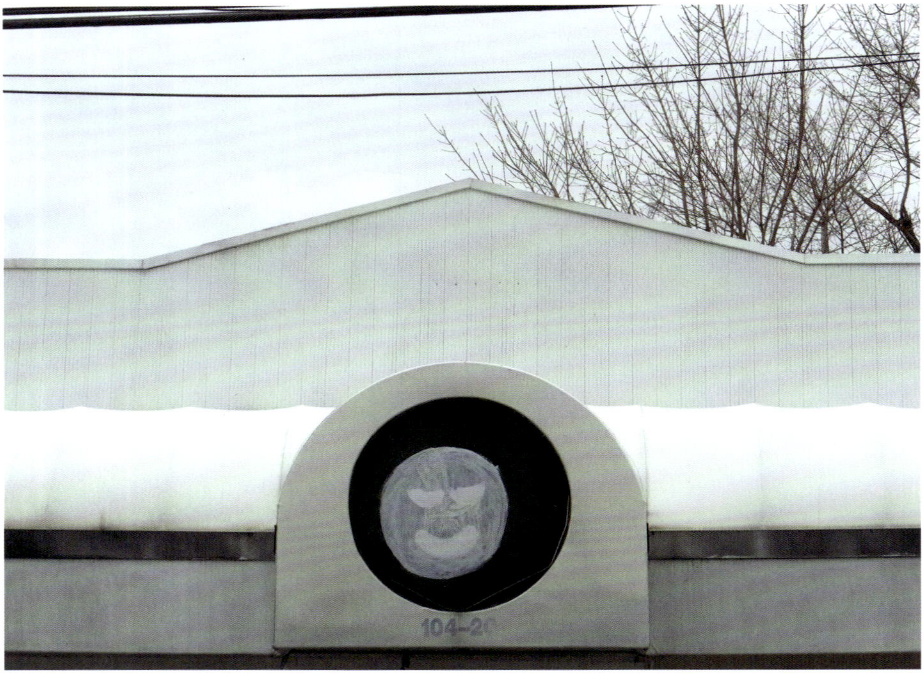
104-20

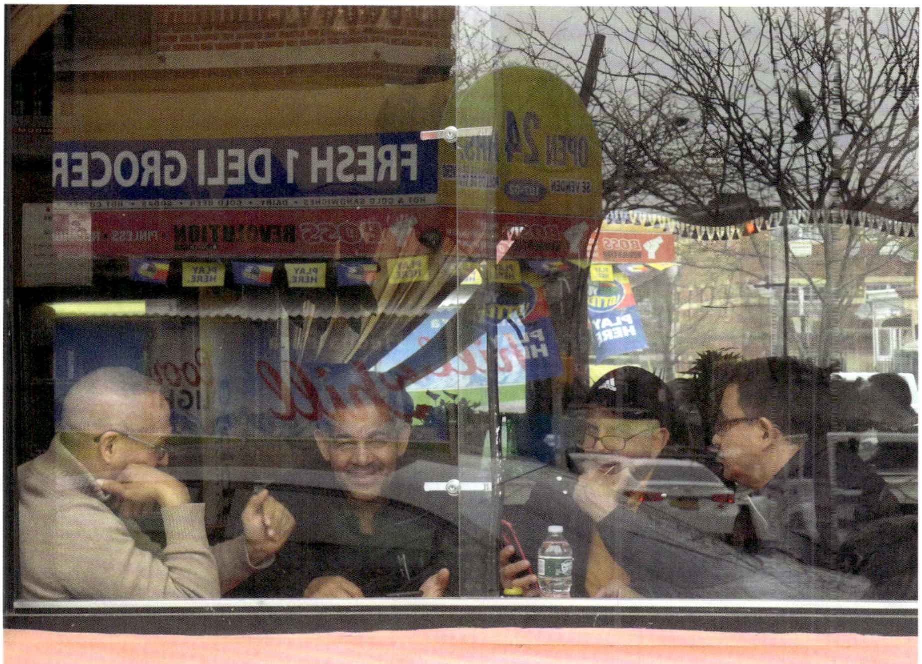
FRESH 1 DELI GROCER
PLAY HERE

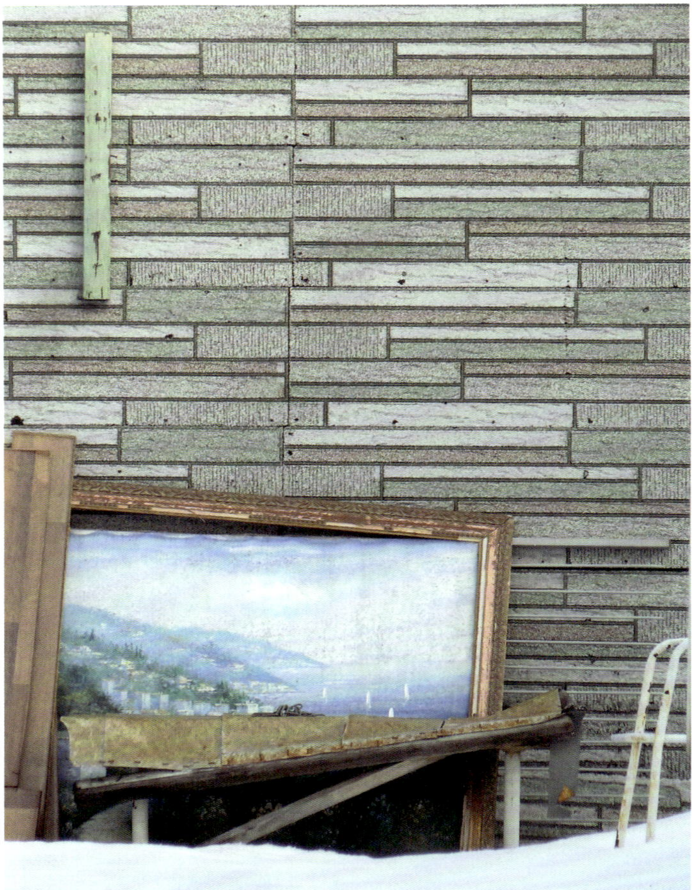

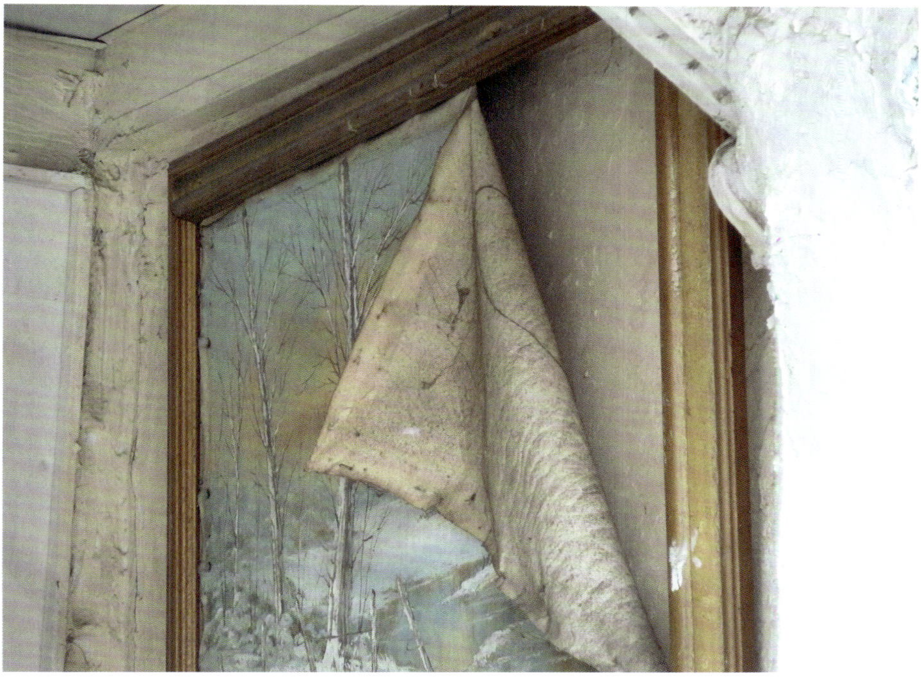

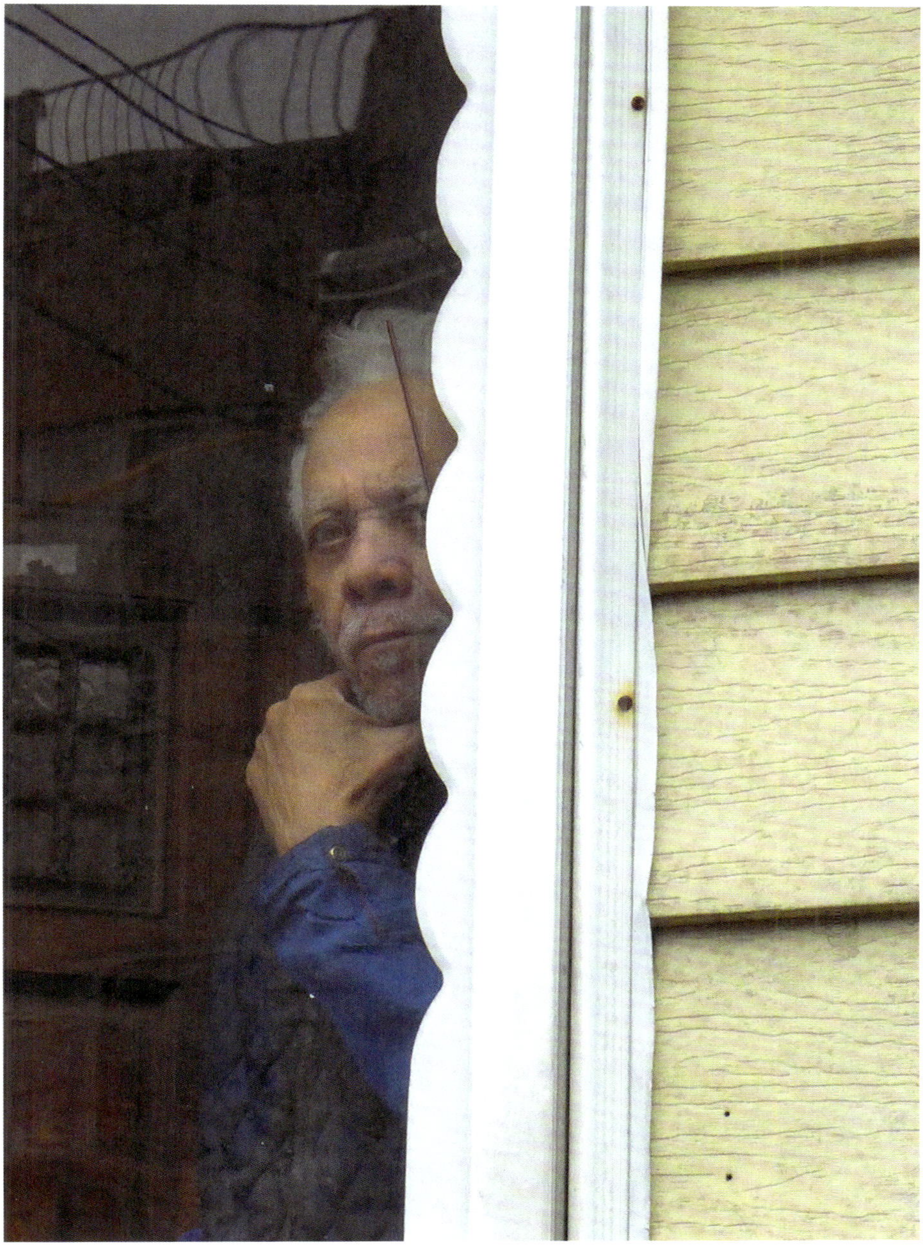

Many thanks to Anders Goldfarb,
Adam Harrison Levy, Howard Gotfryd,
Sabrina Mandanici, Melanie Einzig,
and to my family and friends for their
invaluable guidance, contributions,
encouragement, and support in realizing
this project.